# CONTEMPLATION OF THE HOLY MYSTERIES AND THE RISING OF THE DIVINE LIGHTS

## Also available from Anqa Publishing

*Divine Sayings: 101 Ḥadīth Qudsī*,
by Ibn ʿArabī
Translated by Stephen Hirtenstein and Martin Notcutt

*The Universal Tree and the Four Birds: al-Ittiḥād al-kawnī*,
by Ibn ʿArabī
Translated by Angela Jaffray

*A Prayer for Spiritual Elevation and Protection: al-Dawr al-aʿlā*,
by Ibn ʿArabī
Study, translation, transliteration and Arabic text
by Suha Taji-Farouki

*The Four Pillars of Spiritual Transformation: Ḥilyat al-abdāl*
by Ibn ʿArabī
Translated by Stephen Hirtenstein

*The Unlimited Mercifier: the Spiritual Life and Thought of Ibn ʿArabī*
Stephen Hirtenstein

*Ibn ʿArabi and Modern Thought:*
*The History of Taking Metaphysics Seriously*
Peter Coates

*The Nightingale in the Garden of Love: the Poems of Üftade*
by Paul Ballanfat
Translated from French by Angela Culme-Seymour

*Beshara and Ibn ʿArabi:*
*A Movement of Sufi Spirituality in the Modern World*
Suha Taji-Farouki

*The Teachings of a Perfect Master:*
*An Islamic Saint for the Third Millennium*
Henry Bayman

*Ibn al-ʿArabi and the Sufis*
Binyamin Abrahamov

Muḥyīddīn Ibn ʿArabī

# CONTEMPLATION OF THE HOLY MYSTERIES AND THE RISING OF THE DIVINE LIGHTS

*Mashāhid al-asrār al-qudsiyya wa maṭāliʿ al-anwār al-ilāhiyya*

TRANSLATED FROM THE ARABIC BY
CECILIA TWINCH AND PABLO BENEITO

Based on the annotated critical edition by
Souad Hakim and Pablo Beneito

ANQA PUBLISHING • OXFORD

Published by Anqa Publishing
PO Box 1178
Oxford OX2 8YS, UK

www.anqa.co.uk



First published, 2001
First paperback edition, 2008



A CIP catalogue record for this book is available from the British Library

ISBN 978 1 905937 02 8

Jacket design by Gerard Lennox

Back cover: Ibn 'Arabī's signature
(courtesy of the Beshara School, Scotland)

The assistance of Beshara Publications in the production of this book is gratefully acknowledged.

# Contents

APPENDICES

# Acknowledgements

We would like to thank sincerely all those who have helped with the translation and production of this edition, in particular Stephen Hirtenstein, Sara Hirtenstein, Michael Tiernan, Judy Kearns, Jane Clark, Rosemary Brass, Richard Twinch, and especially Souad Hakim, who has been a constant source of inspiration and help.

# Introduction

*"Take it with strength and make it known to everyone you see . . ."*

Muḥyīddīn Ibn 'Arabī makes it clear that the inspiration to write the *Contemplation of the Holy Mysteries* came from an extremely elevated level.[1] The first instruction that occurred to him concerning the book was "Take it with strength and make it known to everyone you see".[2] This indicates its universal relevance, even though it consists of what may appear to be very private visions and conversations with his innermost Reality. He was also told to verify it for himself and to scrutinize it carefully, implying that it requires close attention in order for its meaning to unfold and become realized.

The *Contemplations*[3] deals with perennial questions such as the nature of existence, our relationship with the all-encompassing Reality, the limits by which we define ourselves and the Truth, and the way to happiness. Ibn 'Arabī makes known the meaning and value of the human being, who is the secret of existence and the purpose of creation. He is told, "If it were not for you, the mysteries would not exist nor would the lights shine."[4]

Between the mystery of what is unseen and the clarity of what is made manifest, between majesty and beauty, compulsion and freedom, awe and intimacy, the Fire and the Garden, a line is drawn that allows for the arising of a unified perspective which

1. He states that it is from the hidden, divine Identity (*huwiyya*). See Ibn 'Arabī's own preface to the book summarized in Appendix 2.

2. See Appendix 2.

3. The title is abbreviated to *Contemplations*. See pp. 21–2, n. 1.

4. Contemplation 6.

encompasses all apparent duality. Interspersed with visions of incredible beauty and wonder, and the promise of eternal happiness, is the warning: pass beyond the forms of images to their meaning, act appropriately and be vigilant.

## *Spiritual journey:*
## *"Rise beyond and you will discover."*[5]

The book consists of fourteen visions or contemplations, each of which is linked to the rising of a star. It begins with "the contemplation of existence as the star of direct vision rises" and continues in an ascending journey to "the contemplation of the light of argument as the star of justice rises", when the traveller arrives at the Day of Judgement. In this ascending journey, the rising of each star heralds a new revelation appearing in the heart of the contemplator.

The style of the *Contemplations* is similar, in this respect, to a later visionary account written by Ibn 'Arabī, the *Kitāb al-Isrā'* or *The Book of the Night Journey*.[6] In fact, Ibn 'Arabī's close disciple, Ibn Sawdakīn, points out in his commentary that the two works are inseparable. Both accounts consist of a sequence of events which follow one another in an ascending series of steps: in the *Contemplations*, each vision refers back to the previous one and leads on to the following.[7]

Similarly, both books have a connection to the Quranic Sura of the Star, which begins, "By the star, when it sets".[8] According to Ibn Sawdakīn's commentary, Ibn 'Arabī relates this to a story in the Quran that tells of Abraham's seeking for the Reality which is permanent.[9] Abraham looked to the heavens, seeing first a star,

5. Contemplation 5.

6. See M. Chodkiewicz, *An Ocean Without Shore*, pp. 78–9.

7. S. Hakim and P. Beneito noted this point in their introduction to the Spanish/Arabic translation and edition, *Las Contemplaciones de los Misterios*, p. XIII.

8. Quran, Sura (or Chapter) 53, verse 1 (Q. 53: 1).

9. See Chodkiewicz, *Ocean*, p. 156, n. 10.

followed by the moon and then the sun. As each celestial body set, he concluded, "I love not those that set" and then became free of his attachment to partial and ephemeral things, turning his attention to and worshipping only the single, essential Truth which is the source of all things.[10] This detachment from everything transitory, and attachment only to the origin of all existence, is an underlying theme of the *Contemplations*, for, as Ibn 'Arabī says in his epilogue:

> The one who stays with the image is lost, and the one who rises from the image to the reality is rightly guided.[11]

The Sura of the Star in the Quran continues with a description of the Prophet Muhammad's Night Journey and the connection to the *Contemplations* can be seen clearly in the verse, "He saw some of the greatest signs of his Lord."[12] As Ibn 'Arabī explains elsewhere, the purpose of spiritual ascension is not to reach God – for He is never apart from us – but simply for Him to show some of His wonders and indications.[13] He writes:

> [God] says, "I only made him journey by night in order that he see the signs, not [to bring him] to Me: because no place can hold Me and the relation of all places to Me is the same. For I am such that [only] 'the heart of My servant, the man of true faith, encompasses Me', so how could he be 'made to journey to Me' while I am 'with him wherever he is'?!"[14]

10. See Q. 6:76–8. See also C. Twinch, "Penetrating Meaning", *Journal of the Muhyiddin Ibn 'Arabi Society* (hereafter *JMIAS*), XX, p. 70.

11. Manisa manuscript, fol. 82b. See Appendix 1.

12. Q. 53:18. Ibn 'Arabī often quotes the following Quranic verse, "We shall show them our signs on the horizons and in themselves until it becomes clear to them that It is the Real." (Q. 41:53) See also Q. 17:1.

13. See Contemplation 3, n. 8.

14. Ibn 'Arabī, *al-Futūḥāt al-Makkiyya*, vol. III, p. 340; see J. W. Morris, "Ibn 'Arabī's Spiritual Ascension", in M. Chodkiewicz, ed., *Les Illuminations de la Mecque/The Meccan Illuminations*, p. 358.

Even after the recognition of the Real manifesting in all images, signs are indications which specifically "increase knowledge and open the eye of understanding".[15] According to a prophetic tradition often quoted by Ibn ʿArabī, "I was a hidden treasure and I loved to be known, so I created the world . . .". This love to be known is not a static goal but a constantly unfolding revelation.

As the star of unveiling rises in the sixth contemplation, the contemplator is told, "Know that every day seventy thousand mysteries from My Majesty pass through the heart of the knower, never to return . . . You are My mirror, My house and My dwelling-place, My hidden treasure and the seat of My knowledge. If it were not for you, I would not be known or worshipped, I would not be thanked or denied." Yet, if the human being, who has the potential for perfection, were for a moment to imagine that such grandeur could in any way be attributed to his limited self, the divine Reality soon reminds him of his inadequacy:

> The looks remain short, the intellects perplexed, the hearts are blind, the knowers are lost in a desert of bewilderment, and the understandings, plunged into stupefaction, are incapable of grasping the least secret of the revelation of My Grandeur. How then could they encompass it? Your knowledge is scattered dust. Your qualities are nothing. Your reality is only a metaphor in a corner of My being.

Through his direct witnessing of spiritual meanings, Ibn ʿArabī is able to illuminate others with regard to what he has realized in himself. That these meanings are clothed in symbolic forms both reveals their beauty and conceals their magnificence, protecting the sanctity of the meanings as well as the vulnerability of those who consider them:

> As for the saints, they have spiritual journeys in the intermediate world during which they directly witness spiritual

15. Morris, "Ibn ʿArabī's Spiritual Ascension", p. 361.

> realities embodied in forms that have become sensible for the imagination; these [sensible images] convey knowledge of the spiritual realities contained within those forms.[16]

These spiritual realities are the secrets of our innermost self and the journey also is within our own self. The holy mysteries revealed in these contemplations are in one aspect particular to the one to whom they were revealed, for what is revealed to each person is unique to the way they receive it. As Ibn ʿArabī writes in his later account of his spiritual ascension, "Each person has a path that no one else but he travels" which comes "to be through the travelling itself."[17] Not only are these contemplations personal in this sense, but it may seem only appropriate for these meanings to be divulged to someone of equal spiritual understanding. Yet Ibn ʿArabī is clearly aware of the universal value of these revelations, for he is repeatedly told to inform others of what he has seen, ". . . tell the servants what you have seen, so that you awaken their longing for Me and fill them with desire for Me, and you will be a mercy for them."[18]

The necessity to inform others involves not only a reminder but a warning. From the inside, the wall that encircles the Garden of Truth appears as pure mercy in the knowledge of the Divine Unity, while from the outside ignorance makes it appear as threat and punishment. The last contemplation, in particular, shows only a small group who have chosen the path to salvation on the Day of Judgement, yet the emphasis is on the fact that people are punished by no one but themselves[19] and their own limited beliefs. Moreover, Ibn ʿArabī's writings generally stress the all-encompassing Mercy of Being which excludes no one.[20] Hell may

16. Morris, "Ibn ʿArabī's Spiritual Ascension", p. 361.
17. Morris, "Ibn ʿArabī's Spiritual Ascension", p. 373.
18. Contemplation 3.
19. See Contemplation 14.
20. See, for example, S. Hirtenstein, *The Unlimited Mercifier*, pp. 121 and 247, or W. C. Chittick, *The Self-Disclosure of God*, p. 220.

then be seen as the suffering which burns off impurity so that what is real can return to itself. Ibn ʿArabī writes:

> If [God's] Anger were to continue [forever], then the suffering [of the damned] would continue. But it is happiness that continues forever, although the dwellings are different, because God places in each abode [of Paradise and Gehenna] that which comprises the enjoyment of the people of that abode.[21]

At the end of the final contemplation the contemplator is warned that whether he follows what he has been told or not, either way he must perish,[22] that is, he must wake up from the illusion of a separate existence, which he can control according to his lower desires, and acknowledge the singular existence of the Real. Then he must follow the order, that is, persist in being true to his Reality. As Ibn ʿArabī was told by the mysterious youth at the start of his own spiritual ascension:

> You are yourself the cloud veiling your own sun!
> So recognize the essential Reality of your being![23]

Beyond the vicissitudes of all that is transitory, the light that is constant continues to shine:

> When the star of the Real rises and enters into the servant's heart, the heart is illuminated and irradiated. Then bewilderment and fear disappear from the possessor of the heart, and he gives news of his Lord explicitly, through hints, and by means of various modes of informing.[24]

21. See Morris, "Ibn ʿArabī's Spiritual Ascension", p. 367.

22. See Muḥammad Ibn ʿAbd al-Jabbār al-Niffarī, *The Mawāqif and Mukhāṭabāt*, *Mawqif* of the Sea, 6, line 10, p. 31: "If thou perishest in other than Me, thou belongest to that in which thou hast perished," (which implies: "If thou perishest in Me, thou belongest to Me").

23. *Kitāb al-isrā'*, p. 14; see C. Addas, *Quest for the Red Sulphur*, p. 202; Hirtenstein, *Mercifier*, p. 117.

24. *Futūḥāt* III, p. 116; see W. C. Chittick, *The Sufi Path of Knowledge*, p. 215.

## *Muḥyīddīn Ibn ʿArabī*

Also known as the Shaykh al-Akbar, the Greatest Master, Ibn ʿArabī is one of the Islamic tradition's most important writers. He wrote more than 300 works[25] and is most famous for his clear explanation of the unity of existence, which is as relevant now as it was in his own time. His continuing influence has been demonstrated by a worldwide surge of interest over the last thirty years or so.

Ibn ʿArabī was born in Murcia in southern Spain in 1165, at a time when the lands the Arabs called al-Andalus, in the Iberian Peninsula, had already been under Muslim rule for over 450 years. At the age of eight, he moved with his family to Seville, which remained his main home for the next twenty-seven years.

When he was about sixteen, he experienced a strong calling to turn to God and went into retreat. He tells us that he returned to the spiritual path due to a vision where he found himself under the guidance of Jesus, Moses and Muhammad, the prophets of the three major religions stemming from Abraham. This seminal vision hints at the breadth of Ibn ʿArabī's thought, which extends to the meanings brought by all the prophets of these traditions, and brings them into a unified perspective.

Ibn ʿArabī began to study the Quran and the Hadith[26] in earnest and soon came under the instruction of his first spiritual master, al-ʿUryanī. It was in connection with this master that Ibn ʿArabī had the first of his several encounters with Khiḍr, the immortal teacher who imparts hidden mysteries. During his youth Ibn ʿArabī kept company with many spiritual teachers, both in Seville and throughout al-Andalus. He went into retreat on several occasions, and had countless mystical experiences, visions and revelations. During these retreats he would sometimes receive Quranic verses, which would descend in a shower of stars, one of the ways in which

25. According to Osman Yahia, about 700 works are attributed to Ibn ʿArabī, of which approximately 400 are extant. See O. Yahia, *Histoire et classification de l'oeuvre d'Ibn ʿArabī*. See also Hirtenstein, *Mercifier*, pp. 236–7 and Appendix 1.

26. Traditional sayings of the Prophet Muhammad.

the Quran was received by Muhammad himself. He would then have secret conversations with God. He wrote later, "The descent of the Quran into the heart of the servant is the descent of God into him; God then speaks to him 'from his inmost self and in his inmost self'."[27]

In 1193, Ibn 'Arabī left the Iberian Peninsula for the first time and sailed across to North Africa to visit Shaykh 'Abd al-'Azīz al-Mahdawī in Tunis. Mahdawī was himself a disciple of the great shaykh Abū Madyan, for whom Ibn 'Arabī had enormous respect and who appears to have influenced him deeply.[28] Ibn 'Arabī spent almost a year in Tunis in the company of Mahdawī and other great masters, many of whom were also disciples of Abū Madyan.

Whilst in Tunis that year, Ibn 'Arabī entered "God's Vast Earth",[29] or the "Earth of Reality", an intelligible, spiritual realm beyond the senses, in which the real and effective adoration of God takes place: "It is the world that is infinite and has no borders where it would reach an end."[30] From then on, according to his own testimony, Ibn 'Arabī worshipped God in this other dimension as a complete servant to the Real, knowing himself to be the Heir *par excellence* of the Muhammadian knowledge and spirituality.[31]

It was on Ibn 'Arabī's return from Tunis in 1194 that he composed the *Contemplation of the Holy Mysteries*, which is one of his first major works. He was then twenty-nine. In the letter which serves as a preface to the book, Ibn 'Arabī dedicates and addresses

27. *Futūḥāt* III, p. 94. See Addas, *Quest*, p. 91; Hirtenstein, *Mercifier*, pp. 83–4.

28. Even though they did not meet in this world except in the spiritual realm. See Hirtenstein, *Mercifier*, pp. 80–90. See also Addas, *Quest*, pp. 45, 89–90, and "Abu Madyan and Ibn 'Arabi", in S. Hirtenstein and M. Tiernan, eds., *Muhyiddin Ibn 'Arabi: A Commemorative Volume*, pp. 175–6. See also G. Elmore, "The *Uwaysī* Spirit", *JMIAS*, XXVIII, pp. 47–56.

29. See Q. 4:97, 29:56. See also Addas, *Quest*, pp. 117–20, and H. Corbin, *Spiritual Body and Celestial Earth*, pp. 135–43.

30. *Futūḥāt* III, p. 47; see Chittick, *Self-Disclosure*, p. 358.

31. See Hakim and Beneito, *Contemplaciones*, p. IV. See also C. Twinch, "Muḥyiddīn Ibn 'Arabī and the Interior Wisdom", in Alfonso Carmona Gonzalez, ed., *Los dos Horizontes*, 1992, pp. 432–7.

the work to Mahdawī's companions, especially to his own paternal cousin, 'Alī b. al-'Arabī.

For the next few years Ibn 'Arabī continued to travel in Spain and North Africa, spending much of his time in Fez where he had many spiritual experiences, including entry into the abode of light, a spiritual ascension and knowledge that he was the Seal of Muhammadian sainthood. During his spiritual ascension, Ibn 'Arabī was enveloped by the divine lights until all of him became Light. There he attained to the Muhammadian station:

> I received the meaning of all the Divine Names and I saw that they all referred to a single Named and to a unique Essence; this Named was the object of my contemplation and this Essence my very being. I had only journeyed in myself and it was to myself that I had been guided; from that, I knew that I was a pure servant, without the least trace of sovereignty.[32]

In 1200 he left Andalusia definitively for his long journey east. In Marrakesh he had another vision during which he was told to take a certain man from Fez to the East with him. His route took him to Bugia where, after visiting the tomb of Abū Madyan, he had a vision that he was married to "all the stars in heaven, being united to each one with a great spiritual joy. After I had become joined with the stars, I was given the letters [of the alphabet] in spiritual marriage."[33]

After spending more time in Tunis with Mahdawī, Ibn 'Arabī finally left the Islamic West and headed towards Mecca. Significantly, on the way he visited the tomb of Abraham in Hebron and the Dome of the Rock in Jerusalem, before passing through Medina, the birthplace of the Prophet Muhammad on his way to the Ka'ba.

While he was in Mecca, Ibn 'Arabī again received many spiritual openings, which he eventually set down in writing in his enormous work *al-Futūḥāt al-Makkiyya* ("The Meccan Revelations"),

32. See Addas, *Quest*, p. 156; Hirtenstein, *Mercifier*, p. 122.
33. Hirtenstein, *Mercifier*, p. 144; Addas, *Quest*, pp. 178–9.

ostensibly for the benefit of his old friend Mahdawī.[34] He also wrote the *Rūḥ al-quds*, in 1203, in defence of the Sufis of Andalusia, which was again addressed to Mahdawī. It was also in Mecca that he met the beautiful Niẓām, daughter of the keeper of the sanctuary of Abraham, who was the inspiration for his famous book of poetry, *Tarjumān al-ashwāq* ("Interpreter of Ardent Desires").

At this time, Ibn ʿArabī met and befriended Majduddīn Isḥāq b. Yūsuf al-Rūmī, vizier to the Seljuk sultan, and they travelled together, via Iraq, to Anatolia. Later, after the death of Majduddīn, Ibn ʿArabī married his widow and brought up their son, Ṣadruddīn Qūnawī, as his own, taking great care over his education. The latter was to become highly instrumental in the spread of Ibn ʿArabī's teachings through the Islamic world. The great friendship and mutual respect between Ṣadruddīn and the celebrated Persian poet, Jalāluddīn Rūmī,[35] also links two strands of Sufism: although Ibn ʿArabī has been hailed as the pinnacle of the way of knowledge and Rūmī as that of love,[36] as Henry Corbin has pointed out: "Both are inspired by the same theophanic sentiment, the same nostalgia for beauty, and the same revelation of love."[37]

Ibn ʿArabī eventually settled in Damascus in 1223, where he continued to teach and write prolifically. In 1229, he had a vision in which the Prophet Muhammad handed him the book of the *Fuṣūṣ al-ḥikam* ("The Bezels of Wisdom"), a work considered by many to be the quintessence of his teachings. By December 1231 the first draft of the monumental *Futūḥāt al-Makkiyya* had been completed. Ibn ʿArabī remained based in Damascus until his death in 1240, and his tomb there is still much revered.[38]

34. See Hirtenstein, *Mercifier*, pp. 144–7 and 151–3; M. Chodkiewicz, *Seal of the Saints*, p. 53, n. 14; *Futūḥāt* I, pp. 6–9.

35. See, e.g., O. Benaïssa, "Akbarian Teaching in Iran in the 13th–14th Centuries", *JMIAS*, XXVI, p. 96.

36. See, e.g., O. Safi, "Did the Two Oceans Meet?", *JMIAS*, XXVI, pp. 55 ff.

37. H. Corbin, *Creative Imagination in the Sufism of Ibn ʿArabī*, p. 70. For comments on this whole period, see Hirtenstein, *Mercifier*, pp. 173–5 and 238–9.

38. There are now several excellent introductions to Ibn ʿArabī's life and thought: for example, Addas, *Quest* and Hirtenstein, *Mercifier*.

## *This edition*

This edition of the *Contemplation of the Holy Mysteries and the Rising of the Divine Lights* is based on the critical edition with notes by Souad Hakim and Pablo Beneito. The work first appeared in a Spanish/Arabic bilingual edition in Spain in 1994, published as part of a collection of Ibn ʿArabī's works initiated by the Ministry for Culture and Education for the Autonomous Region of Murcia, where Ibn ʿArabī was born. A revised and corrected second edition appeared in 1996.

I was originally asked to translate the book from Spanish into English but soon realized that it was necessary to learn Arabic in order to translate directly from the original text. As I had already been studying Ibn ʿArabī's work in translation for many years and was familiar both with his ideas and with much of his technical vocabulary, it was very exciting finally to be able to read his work in the original. It was also daunting to comprehend the difficulties of translating such a rich and subtle language, where each word contains so many meanings and connotations. It has therefore been of inestimable benefit to work in collaboration with Pablo Beneito and to have the support and help of Souad Hakim.

However, in this edition we have adapted the introduction and notes to make the work more accessible to the non-specialist, English-speaking reader. We recommend that Arabists requiring, for example, folio numbers and further references to works only available in Arabic consult the Spanish/Arabic edition.

The manuscript upon which the translation is based includes a preface and an epilogue. These have not been translated in full but have been summarized in the appendices. Ibn ʿArabī's preface to the *Contemplations* was previously considered as a separate treatise on sainthood and prophecy, entitled *Risāla fī 'l-walāya* ("Treatise on Sainthood").[39] It is written in the form of a letter and Ibn ʿArabī

39. Edited by H. Taher under the title "Sainthood and Prophecy", and published in *Alif*, No. 5, 1985, pp. 7–38; see Addas, *Quest*, pp. 126–9; see also Chodkiewicz, *Seal*, p. 47, n. 2 and index under *Walāya* for other references.

begins by stating that it is addressed to the companions of his teacher, Shaykh ʿAbd al-ʿAzīz al-Mahdawī. However, the text of the fourteen contemplations constitutes the main part of the work and stands by itself. The preface and epilogue may be considered as additions, which both facilitate the reading of the work and defend the authenticity of inspiration, mystical contemplation and conversation with the Real.[40]

In annotating and translating the *Contemplations*, there has been constant recourse to the explanations by Ibn Sawdakīn and Sitt al-ʿAjam, as well as those contained in the brief commentary which appears, by way of appendix, in the source manuscript – and whose authority may be attributed to Ibn ʿArabī himself.[41] Ismāʿīl b. Sawdakīn al-Nūrī (1181–1248) was one of Ibn ʿArabī's closest companions. His name first appears in connection with Ibn ʿArabī on a reading certificate for the *Rūḥ al-quds* in Cairo in 1206 and subsequently appears on numerous other certificates for readings, many of which took place at his house in Aleppo. Besides his commentary on the *Contemplation of the Holy Mysteries* (*Mashāhid al-asrār*), Ibn Sawdakīn wrote commentaries on the *Kitāb al-Isrā'*, with which it is closely linked, and the *Kitāb al-Tajalliyāt*. In these commentaries, he informs us, he simply wrote down what Ibn ʿArabī told him. They are therefore an invaluable aid to the understanding of the text.

Sitt al-ʿAjam bint al-Nafīs b. Abū 'l-Qāsim (died about 1288) was a great mystic from Baghdad. Her commentary on the *Contemplations*[42] was written less than fifty years after Ibn ʿArabī's death, and she begins it with an account of a vision during which she conversed with Ibn ʿArabī before a company of prophets. She therefore also received information from Ibn ʿArabī about the *Contemplations*, but in a visionary way.[43]

40. See Hakim and Beneito, *Contemplaciones*, p. XIII.

41. For information about the manuscripts, see Appendix 1.

42. S. Hakim and B. Aladdin have recently published a critical edition of this work. See Bibliography.

43. See Chodkiewicz, *Ocean*, p. 79 and pp. 156–7, n. 9.

## *The style and symbolism of the Contemplations*

The *Contemplations* evokes the style of two works by one of Ibn ʿArabī's predecessors in the Islamic mystical tradition, the *Mawāqif – Book of Spiritual Stayings* and the *Mukhātabāt – Book of Spiritual Addresses* by Niffarī (d. 965), the inspired Sufi master whom Ibn ʿArabī himself refers to in his preface as "the author of the *Mawāqif*".[44] Although the speech in Niffarī's works is mainly from the side of the Divine, there are also conversations and narrative sections, for example in the *Mawqif* of "Who art thou and who am I?"[45] The *Contemplations* differs mainly by the continuity of its narrative sequence, but there is a striking similarity to the author of the *Mawāqif*'s use of expressions such as "And then He said to me . . .".[46] In order to avoid excessive repetition in our translation we have omitted some of these, enclosing each statement within inverted commas on a new line instead. The Arabic manuscript has no punctuation and the text runs on almost continuously, as was common at that time. Modern punctuation and layout of the text allow for the required pause between statements.

It should be emphasized that the contemplations are visions of the Real in a holy place. They are not passive contemplations, but active in the sense of seeing with one's own eyes and then bearing witness. This active response of witnessing is reflected in the reply to the question "Am I not your Lord?" alluded to in the first contemplation,[47] and in the need to bear witness to one's deeds on the Day of Judgement, or on the day when Truth is revealed, exemplified in the final contemplation. As Ibn ʿArabī points out in the *Fuṣūṣ al-ḥikam*, every person is conscious of their own state of soul: "The human being has an intuitive perception of himself

44. Niffarī, *Mawāqif*. See Hakim and Beneito, *Contemplaciones*, p. XIII.

45. See Niffarī, *Mawāqif*, p. 80.

46. Most lines in the *Mawāqif* begin "And He said to me", although this has been omitted in translation. Notice, for example, *Mawqif* 13, line 7, which begins "And He said to me, 'When I make you contemplate . . .'", translated as "When I cause thee to witness . . .".

47. See Contemplation 1, n. 36.

whatever excuse he may give."[48] The witnessing described in the contemplations is not just seeing but actively acknowledging.[49]

From the very first contemplation, Ibn ʿArabī's frequent use of opposites and apparent paradox is in evidence. Seen from one point of view, a particular statement is valid, but at another level of understanding its opposite is true. For Ibn ʿArabī, the singularity of Truth originates at the point where the opposites are united, and then the Truth expresses itself in all its diverse forms.

The science of letters in Islamic cosmology is fundamental to understanding the significance of number within the book and in particular the fact that there are fourteen contemplations. As Pablo Beneito and Souad Hakim have pointed out in their introduction to the Spanish/Arabic edition of the *Contemplations*, the number fourteen is related to the cosmos, the Perfect Man and the Quran – in particular the opening sura.[50] For Ibn ʿArabī, there is a direct analogy between the Breath of the All-Compassionate through which the world becomes manifest and the human breath by means of which the twenty-eight letters of the Arabic alphabet become articulated.[51] As God speaks the Divine Word, "Be!", to each thing He wishes to manifest, He has compassion on what each thing is in itself, and it becomes, according to how it is.

Each letter has its own numerical value and is connected to a day in the lunar cycle, a level of existence, a Divine Name. In fact, Ibn ʿArabī says, "It is not like people think, that the mansions of the Moon represent the models of the letters; it is the twenty-eight sounds which determine the lunar mansions."[52]

48. Q. 75: 14–15. See also Ibn ʿArabī, *The Wisdom of the Prophets*, translated by T. Burckhardt/A. Culme-Seymour, p. 131.

49. See Chittick, *Sufi Path*, pp. 227–8.

50. See Hakim and Beneito, *Contemplaciones*, pp. XVIII–XX. On the significance of the number fourteen, see also Ibn ʿArabī, *The Seven Days of the Heart*, translated and presented by P. Beneito and S. Hirtenstein, pp. 9–19, 145–55.

51. See Hirtenstein, *Mercifier*, Chapter 16; Chittick, *Sufi Path*, pp. 128–9 and *Self-Disclosure*, pp. xxviii–xxxii.

52. See T. Burckhardt, *Mystical Astrology According to Ibn ʿArabī*, p. 35, and the diagram on pp. 32–3.

There are fourteen solar and fourteen lunar letters in the Arabic alphabet. This total of twenty-eight is also the number of days in the lunar cycle, whose fourteenth night corresponds to the full moon.[53] Ibn ʿArabī refers to this full moon in his *Tarjumān al-ashwāq*: "Between Adhriʿāt and Buṣrā a maid of fourteen rose to my sight like a full moon."[54] In the accompanying commentary, Ibn ʿArabī explains that the maid of fourteen means the perfect soul. He also explains that four is the most perfect number, and ten consists of four numbers (1 + 2 + 3 + 4) and fourteen is 4 + 10.

Fourteen, as twice seven, represents the seven heavens and the seven earths of Islamic cosmology, and therefore the Divine Throne which encompasses all the worlds.[55] In the epilogue to the *Contemplations*, Ibn ʿArabī refers to the Quranic verse, "God is the One who created seven heavens and of the earth a similar number. Through them His command descends so that you may know that God has power over everything and that God comprehends everything in His knowledge."[56] Ibn ʿArabī then adds the declaration made by Ibn ʿAbbās: "If I explained this verse, you would stone me!" There is a correspondence between the witnessing of the fourteen contemplations which Ibn ʿArabī recounts and these fourteen heavens and earths, for according to a traditional saying of the Prophet Muhammad: "I bring before you as witnesses the seven heavens and the seven earths."[57]

The perfect self is related to the full moon and is also called the Perfect Man or the Complete Human Being (*al-insān al-kāmil*). Just as the Breath of the All-Compassionate is the Reality of Realities at a cosmic level, so the Reality of Muhammad is the Reality of

53. See Hakim and Beneito, *Contemplaciones*, pp. 3–4, n. 2.

54. See the *Tarjumān al-ashwāq* (Interpreter of Ardent Desires), translated by R. A. Nicholson, poem XL, pp. 124–5.

55. See Hakim and Beneito, *Contemplaciones*, p. XVIII. See also Burckhardt, *Mystical Astrology*, pp. 12–13.

56. Q. 65: 12.

57. Collected by Aḥmad b. Ḥanbal (Musnad, V, 135). See A. J. Wensinck, *Concordance de la tradition musulmane*. See Hakim and Beneito, *Contemplaciones*, pp. 3–4, n. 2.

Realities at a human level, encompassing in a single reality all the individual possibilities of human perfection. Muhammad therefore represents the principle of the perfection of the human being.

The enigmatic letters *ṭā'–hā'*, which form the first verse of the twentieth sura of the Quran and which are mentioned in the twelfth contemplation, are traditionally considered to be one of the names of the Prophet Muhammad.[58] The Quranic passage is as follows: "*Ṭā'–Hā'*. We have not revealed the Quran so that you suffer . . .".[59] On adding up the numerical values which correspond to these two letters (*ṭā'* = 9, *hā'* = 5) the sum of fourteen is obtained. Moreover, there are fourteen enigmatic letters which appear at the beginning of many suras of the Quran.[60]

According to Ibn ʿArabī, the Quran is the Word of God and he explains the relationship of the Quran to the human being when he writes, "The Total Man, according to the essential reality, is the incomparable Quran descended from the Presence of Itself into the Presence of the One who gives existence . . .".[61] The Perfect Human Being summarizes the whole of existence, from the lowest to the highest degree. He both encompasses the worlds and is a copy of the world.[62] All that the 114 suras of the Quran contain in detail are summarized in the opening sura, the *Fātiḥa*, which contains seven verses and is also referred to as "the seven doubled" (*al-sabʿ al-mathānī*). The *Fātiḥa* is regarded as the perfect prayer and is repeated in all the ritual prayers of Islam. Ibn ʿArabī writes, "It is the Seven Doubled Ones, for it includes the [seven] attributes [of the Essence]."[63] The seven attributes of the Essence

58. See Contemplation 12, n. 15 and Hakim and Beneito, *Contemplaciones*, p. XIX.

59. Q. 20: 1–2.

60. See Hakim and Beneito, *Contemplaciones*, p. XIX. See also *The Holy Qur'ān*, text, translation and commentary by A. Yusuf Ali, Appendix I, pp. 118–20, and Chodkiewicz, *Illuminations*, p. 425.

61. *Kitāb al isfār ʿan natā'ij al-asfār*, edited and translated by D. Gril under the title *Le Dévoilement des Effets du Voyage*, p. 22. See P. Lory, "The Symbolism of Letters and Language", *JMIAS*, XXIII, p. 37. See also M. Chodkiewicz, "Une introduction à la lecture des *Futūḥāt Makkiyya*", *Illuminations*, pp. 42–3.

62. See Contemplation 12, n. 15.

63. Ibn ʿArabī, *Tanazzulāt*, p. 95; see Chodkiewicz, *Ocean*, p. 111.

are that It is Knowing, Willing, Able, Living, Speaking, Seeing and Hearing.[64]

It is significant that Ibn ʿArabī wrote the *Contemplations* shortly after his declaration in Tunis, which shocked Mahdawī and his companions: "I am the Quran and the seven doubled."[65] When Ibn ʿArabī explains prayer, making particular reference to the *Fātiḥa*, he quotes the revealed word of God according to which prayer is shared between God and his servant.[66] With regard to God, he writes elsewhere, "He is as though He doubled/praised Himself, and He is the praiser and the praised."[67] The attributes which belong to God are therefore made manifest in the servant and in the sixth contemplation, the Divine Reality informs the contemplator, "I have brought into being in you the attributes and qualities by which I wish you to know Me."[68]

The seventy veils lifted in the third contemplation along with the naming of the Stone, the 70,000 mysteries referred to in the sixth contemplation along with the risings and witnessings equal to the consonants and vowels of the alphabet, the sailing on the ocean into the seventh millennium in the ninth contemplation before diving for the keys to the treasury of the Essence – all of these emphasize the significance of the science of numbers and letters in this richly symbolic work, where the heavenly bodies are seen as divine signs on the horizon pointing to the wisdom waiting to be revealed within ourselves.

64. See Contemplation 9, n. 29. See also Hirtenstein, *Mercifier*, p. 215.

65. (*anā al-qur'ān wa al-sabʿ al-mathānī*); see Q. 15:87. See also Addas, *Quest*, p. 119, and for the full poem from which the quotation is taken, see Hirtenstein, *Mercifier*, p. 88.

66. "I have divided prayer between Me and My servant into two halves, one being due to Me, and the other to My servant; and My servant will receive that for which he asks." See Chapter of Muhammad in the *Fuṣūṣ al-ḥikam*, in Burckhardt/Culme-Seymour, *Wisdom*, p. 127, and *Ismail Hakki Bursevi's translation of and commentary on the Fusus al-hikam by Muhyiddin Ibn ʿArabi*, trans. B. Rauf, p. 1097.

67. See Ibn ʿArabī, *Wird*, fol. 8, Arabic (translated in Beneito and Hirtenstein, *Seven Days*, p. 41), the Sunday morning prayer.

68. See Contemplation 6.

## *The Arabic language*

Each word in Arabic contains a wealth of connotations which are impossible to confine within a word-for-word translation. Yet despite these limitations, some of the original meanings of the words seep through and are communicated. Even if taken only at the level of poetic prose, the beauty of some of the images is able to reach beyond linguistic and cultural context to resonate with the profound mysteries within each of us.

In order to facilitate ease of reading, only a few Arabic transliterations have been included in the text itself. However, since there has been a tradition of using Arabic words in European translations of Ibn ʻArabī's work, additional transliterations have sometimes been included in the notes for the benefit of those non-Arabists who have become familiar with some of Ibn ʻArabī's precise, technical vocabulary. Besides the notes drawn from the commentaries by Ibn Sawdakīn and Sitt al-ʻAjam, a minimum of notes have been included to clarify certain points that would have been fairly obvious to a reader who shared the same historical, cultural and linguistic context as Ibn ʻArabī but which may not be so obvious now, particularly to those without any background in Islam and who have little or no knowledge of Arabic.

It is hoped that these will provide a few keys to the ocean of meanings contained in this book and at least indicate some of its many possible levels of interpretation. Nevertheless, due to the clarity of its source, this book of the *Contemplations*, like other writings by Ibn ʻArabī, remains ever open to fresh contemplation, allowing new and unexpected meanings to emerge.

*Oxford* *Cecilia Twinch*
*June 2000*

# CONTEMPLATIONS

## TRANSLATION AND NOTES

# From Ibn ʿArabī's Preface

This is the treatise entitled *Contemplation of the Holy Mysteries and the Rising of the Divine Lights.*[1] We have extracted it for you from the guarded treasures in the hidden depths of eternity without beginning, which are preserved from the accidents arising from desires and defects. I have collected in it fourteen contemplations:

- Contemplation of the light of existence
  as the star of direct vision rises.
- Contemplation of the light of taking
  as the star of affirmation rises.
- Contemplation of the light of the veils
  as the star of strong backing rises.
- Contemplation of the light of intuition
  as the star of transcendence rises.
- Contemplation of the light of silence
  as the star of negation rises.
- Contemplation of the light of elevation
  as the star of unveiling rises.
- Contemplation of the light of the leg
  as the star of the summons rises.
- Contemplation of the light of the rock
  as the star of the sea rises.
- Contemplation of the light of the rivers
  as the star of degrees rises.
- Contemplation of the light of perplexity
  as the star of non-existence rises.
- Contemplation of the light of divinity
  as the star of *lām–alif* rises.
- Contemplation of the light of uniqueness
  as the star of servanthood rises.
- Contemplation of the light of the support
  as the star of singularity rises.
- Contemplation of the light of argument
  as the star of justice rises.

# *Note*

1. *Mashāhid* (plural of *mashhad*) is here translated as "contemplation" but it could equally well be translated as "witnessings". The term *mashhad*, the "place-name" of the root *sh–h–d* (meaning to witness, see with one's own eyes, experience personally, bear witness, testify, give evidence) means "the (meeting) place (or place of assembly) in which one is present or in which one witnesses something", and hence, "contemplative state". In English, the emphasis is on the singular, active experience of contemplation, so the title has been translated as the *Contemplation of the Holy Mysteries*, although the book consists of fourteen separate contemplations or visions within a unified experience. The word *asrār* may be translated as "mysteries" or "secrets".

   The word *maṭāliʿ* (plural of *maṭlaʿ*) refers to the rising or ascension of a celestial body. As we do not talk of plural "risings" of the sun and moon in English, this has been translated as "rising" in the singular.

# 1

# Contemplation of the Light of Existence (*wujūd*) as the Star of Direct Vision (*ʿiyān*) rises

IN THE NAME OF GOD,
THE COMPASSIONATE, THE MERCIFUL

The Real made me contemplate the light of existence[1] as the star of direct vision[2] rose, and He asked me, "Who are you?"

I replied, "Apparent non-existence."[3]

Then He said to me, "And how can non-existence change into existence? If you were not an existing [entity], your existence would not be possible and real."[4]

I replied, "That is why I said apparent non-existence, since hidden non-existence does not have real existence."[5]

Then He said to me, "If [one considers that] the first existence is identical to the second existence, then there is not a preceding non-existence, nor a contingent existence.[6] However, it is established that you are contingent."[7]

"The first existence is not the same as the second."[8]

"The first existence is like the existence of the universals, and the second existence is like the existence of the particulars."

"Non-existence is real and there is nothing else; and existence is real and there is nothing else."

I agreed, saying, "That is so."

Then He said to me, "Are you a Muslim[9] by mere tradition or do you have your own standard of judgement?"[10]

I answered, "I am not a [blind] imitator nor do I follow my own [rational] opinion."

He said to me, "Then you are no thing."[11]

I said to Him, "I am the thing without likeness and You are the thing with likeness."[12]

He said, "What you say is true."

Then He told me, "You are not a thing, nor have you been a thing, nor are you according to a thing."

"That is so," I replied, "since if I were a thing, perception would be able to apprehend me;[13] if I were according to a thing, the three relationships[14] would apply to me, and if I were thing I would have an opposite, but I have no opposite."[15]

Then I said to Him, "I exist in the parts,[16] although I do not exist,[17] so I am named without name, qualified without quality and described without description, and this constitutes my perfection. However, You are named by the name, qualified by the quality and described by the description, and this constitutes Your perfection."[18]

Then He said to me, "Only the non-existent knows the existent."

"Only what is existent knows the existent as it is in reality. Existence is from Me, not from you,[19] but it is in you, not in Me."[20]

Then He said to me, "Whoever finds you finds Me and whoever loses you loses Me."[21]

"Whoever finds you loses Me and whoever loses you finds Me."[22]

"Whoever loses me finds Me[23] and whoever has found Me does not lose Me."[24]

"Finding and losing are yours, not Mine."[25]

Then He said to me, "Every [kind of] limited and relative existence is yours and all absolute and unlimited existence belongs to Me."

"Relative existence belongs to Me not to you."

"Differentiated existence, which is Mine, is through you, and integrated existence, which is yours, is through Me."[26]

"And vice versa."

Then He said to me, "Primordial pre-existence is not [really] existence,[27] but below it[28] is true existence."

"Existence is through Me,[29] it comes from Me[30] and it is Mine."[31]

"Existence comes from Me, but it is not through Me, nor is it Mine."[32]

"Existence is not through Me, nor does it come from Me."[33]

Then He said, "If you find Me you will not see Me[34] but you will see Me if you lose Me."[35]

"Finding is losing Me and losing is finding Me. Were you able to discover taking,[36] then you would know real existence."

# *Notes*

(IS) = Ibn Sawdakin; (SA) = Sitt al-ʿAjam. See Introduction, p.12.

1 "[Ibn ʿArabī] is using [the term] 'the light of existence' (*nūr al-wujūd*) analogically, since light [like existence] manifests itself and manifests other than itself, being perceptible [as light] at the same time as being the means by which perception takes place, whereas darkness is perceptible but one cannot perceive by means of it." (IS)

To understand Ibn ʿArabī's notion of existence, it is necessary to bear in mind that in Arabic, *wujūd* ("existence", "Being") from the root *w-j-d*, also means "finding" or "discovery".

Most of the chapters begin with the words: *ashhadanī 'l-ḥaqq bi-mashhad nūr . . . wa ṭulūʿ najm . . .*, meaning: "The Real (the Truth or God, *al-ḥaqq*) caused me to witness in the place of witnessing of the light of . . . and the rising of the star of . . .". For ease of reading we have simplified the translation.

2 The rising (*ṭulūʿ*) of the star of direct vision "that is, the contemplation (*mashhad*) of existence from the place of manifestation (*maẓhar*)." (IS)

"Direct vision" (*ʿiyān*) is immediate knowledge, seeing with one's own eyes, the testimony of the eyewitness.

3 "Apparent non-existence" or "apparent nothingness" (*al-ʿadam al-ẓāhir*), "that is, apparent to You [the Real], but not to me [the servant]." (IS)

4 "That is, if you were not existent for Me [God], your existence would not be real for you [the servant]." (IS)

Ibn ʿArabī uses the term *ʿabd*, "servant", to refer to the ontological condition of the human being, which is synonymous with *khalq*, "creation", and in contrast to *al-ḥaqq*, God as Truth or Reality.

5 "Apparent non-existence", "potential non-being" or "non-existence which manifests" is the possible (*mumkin*), whilst "non-existence or nothingness which does not manifest" (*al-ʿadam al-bāṭin*) is impossible. See S. Hakim, *al-Muʿjam al-ṣūfī*, "*al-ʿadam al-imkānī*" (potential non-being), "*al-ʿadam al-muṭlaq*" (absolute non-being) and "*ʿayn thābita*" (established potentiality/fixed entity).

6 "[Ibn ʿArabī] is pointing out that the intelligibility of existence is one." (IS)

The term "first existence" refers to the pre-eternal existence in the divine omniscience, whilst "second existence" refers to existence in the concrete individual essences (*aʿyān*).

7 "That is, your consciousness of yourself truly exists." (IS) The contingent or "newly-happening" depends on the eternal or "that which always was" for its existence.

8 This statement, and the two following ones, are preceded by "Then He said to me" in the original Arabic text. The Arabic manuscript has no punctuation and the text runs on almost continuously, as was common at that time. Modern punctuation and layout of the text allow for the required pause. Throughout the text, we have indicated the omission of "And He said to me" between statements by beginning a new line and by using opening and closing quotation marks. See Introduction, p.13.

9 Literally "muslim" means "in submission [to the will of God]".

10 Neither the blind imitators, nor those who follow their own rational judgement succeed in *discovering* the truth. The negative response to both possibilities indicates that this spiritual station of the contemplations, which comes after entry into the station of knowledge and the unveiling of mysteries beyond comprehension by the intellect, is above erudition and argument. (SA)

11 The possible is not a thing (i.e. it is nothing, non-existent), for it has no actual, but only virtual, existence. See n.15 below.

12 The term *mithliyya*, "likeness", derived from the word *mithl*, "like", relates to Q.42:11. In this verse there is a phrase which, according to Ibn ʿArabī, may be read in two ways: "There is not anything like Him", or, "there is nothing like His likeness." (The compound *ka-mithl* may either be understood as a single preposition, whose second element only reinforces the meaning of the first – in which case it would simply be translated as "like" – or else, as a compound of preposition and noun, in which case *ka*, "like", would be the prefixed preposition and *mithl*, "likeness" or "similar", the noun.)

For Ibn ʿArabī (who now has in mind the second reading), this verse affirms the likeness with relation to God (that is, the existence of the similar to Him), whilst denying any likeness with respect to His likeness (to which nothing is similar). This likeness which has no likeness is the Universal Man created "according to the form of the Compassionate". See P. Beneito, *El Secreto de los Nombres de Dios*, p.63, n.3.

In his commentary on this expression, Ibn Sawdakīn says: "I am associated with You in existence, but You are not associated with me [that is, you do not participate with me] in non-existence . . . It is as if one said: 'I am Your similar, whilst You are not my similar'."

13 That is, it would be possible to perceive me.

14 "The three relationships: (1) rational opinion, (2) existence in the exterior, and (3) existence in the essential reality. When the gnostic (*'ārif*) experiences the annihilation of multiple existence, he necessarily has to divest himself of relationships." (SA)

15 "'Not to be [any]thing' or '[to be] no thing' (*lā shay'*) can only be opposed to the existence of the Creator, but that which 'is no thing' cannot, in any way, be opposed to the existence of the possible, since what we call 'possible' (*mumkin*) is the same as what we call 'no thing'." (IS)

16 "That is, in the particulars and in everything." (IS)

17 "Because everything that creates the possible is attributed to the Real (*al-ḥaqq*)." (IS)

18 The attribution of the things to the servant in a metaphorical way constitutes his perfection in the station of servanthood, whilst their attribution to the Real (*al-ḥaqq*) as verified fact is His perfection. (IS)

19 "That is, the existence of the 'individual essences' (*a'yān*)." (IS)

20 "That is, the existence of the knowledges (*ma'ārif*)." (IS)

21 "Because the divine perfection only manifests in this Adamic form." (IS)

22 Whoever attributes existence to you loses Me, but whoever does not attribute existence to you finds Me. (IS)

23 An allusion to the famous saying of Abū Bakr al-Ṣiddīq, "the Veracious": "[To realize] the impossibility of attaining knowledge (*idrāk*) is [itself] knowledge." (IS) See also Contemplation 3, nn.16 and 17, Contemplation 6, n.23 and Contemplation 10, n.9.

24 "That is, if he finds Me by means of this existence which has no similar he does not lose Me." (IS)

25 MS. B adds, "Then He said to me, 'Finding and losing are Mine not yours.'"

26 God distributed existence among the created things and the human being reunites the differentiated existence and returns it to God. (SA)

27 Existence in knowledge (the divine primordial foreknowledge) is not differentiated and there is no point in existence except after differentiation. As it is not differentiated, this pre-existence is not really considered to be existence, since true existence is in the visible exterior. (SA)

28 The pronoun "it" refers to the "priority" of the first existence. This means that real or actual existence, since it is apparent, is ontologically inferior to primordial existence.

29 "That is, since the Essence necessitates it." (IS)

30 That is, from My choice. (IS)

31 Or "and it is for My sake." "This is similar to the verse '[I only created the jinn and humankind] that they might worship Me' (Q.51:56), where the reason why God created is explicitly expressed." (IS)

32 ("Nor is it for My sake"), that is, "I did not create existence for My sake," because God is Rich-beyond-Need of the universes. This is a refutation of the doctrine of causality which postulates cause and effect with respect to the creation of the world. (IS)

33 "In the sense that there is no correspondence." (IS) MSS. B and J add *wa-lā lī*: "nor is it Mine", or "nor is it for My sake".

34 "Absolute existence (*al-wujūd al-muṭlaq*) cannot be limited. Yet existence is manifested in actual places of manifestation and every place of manifestation is limited." (IS) See above, n.1.

35 That is, if you leave the limited form and return to the unlimited reality, you will see Me. (IS and SA)

36 This refers to the "taking" mentioned in the Quranic verse: "And when your Lord *took* from the children of Adam – from their loins (literally, 'backs': *ẓuhūr*) – their descendants and made them bear witness to themselves (*ashhada-hum 'alayhim*) [saying] 'Am I not your Lord?', they said 'Yes, indeed (*balā*)! We do bear witness.'" (Q.7:172) See Contemplation 2, nn.1 and 7.

# 2

# Contemplation of the Light of Taking (*akhdh*) as the Star of Affirmation (*iqrār*) rises

IN THE NAME OF GOD,
THE COMPASSIONATE, THE MERCIFUL

The Real made me contemplate the light of [Divine] taking as the star of affirmation rose.[1]

Then He said to me, "Taking is the same as letting go[2] but not everything that is let go of is taken."[3]

"You can find Me[4] but you cannot take hold of me;[5] I can take hold of you but I cannot find you."

"I do not take hold of you nor do I find you."

"I find you, but I do not take hold of you."

Then He said to me, "Taking only occurs from behind,[6] since if it were from in front nobody would go astray."

"I have manifested myself in taking [the servant] and I have hidden Myself in letting [him] go."[7]

"Taking implies three [aspects][8] and everything that exceeds this number is no longer taking."[9]

"[In reality,] I took Myself."

Then He said to me, "Look at the 'inanimate beings' and listen to[10] their glorification of God, for that is their responding 'Yes, indeed!' "[11]

"If I veiled you with the taking[12] [keeping you in this state of extinction without return to subsistence], you would suffer eternal pain in everlasting happiness."

"I only take him [to] whom I have said ['Be!', giving him existence][13] and I have only said ['Be!' to] what is owned [by Me]. Nothing is owned unless it is dominated, and nothing is dominated unless it is confined, and nothing is confined unless it is newly arrived, and nothing arrives newly except the [potential] non-existence."

"I took what was dispersed and united it. I took it from the union and I reunited it. Then I dispersed it and united it [once more],[14] and then there was neither division nor union."

Then He made me contemplate what is above taking, and I saw the Hand.[15] Then the Green Sea[16] poured forth between the Hand and me. I became immersed in it[17] and I saw a tablet.[18] I climbed onto it and [like that] I was saved, since had it not been for [the tablet], I would have perished.

Then the Hand appeared, and behold! the Hand was serving as the shore of that sea, upon which the boats sailed until they arrived at the shore. When they reached it, the Hand pushed them along to a deserted place.[19] The owners of the boats disembarked carrying with them pearls, jewels and coral; but as soon as they stepped onto dry land, these all turned into ordinary stones.

I said to Him, "How does one keep the pearls as pearls, the jewels as jewels and the coral as coral?"

He said, "When you come out of the sea, take away with you some sea-water, for whilst the water remains, pearls, jewels and coral will continue in that state; but if the water dries up, they will turn into ordinary stones. In the Sura of the Prophets[20] I have made its secret clear."

And so I took [some] of that water to carry with me, and when I reached the deserted land I saw a verdant garden[21] in the middle of that arid place. I was told, "Come in."

I went in and I saw its blossoms and radiant flowers,[22] its birds and its fruit. When I stretched out my hand to eat of those fruits, the water dried up and the precious gems were transformed [into ordinary stones].

Then [I heard] the voice which reprimanded me saying, "Throw away the fruit that you have in your hand!"[23]

I threw it away, and immediately the water flowed again and the gems regained their former state.

Then He said to me, "Go to the boundary of the garden."

So I went there and found a desert.[24] "Cross it", He said. So I crossed it and [on the way] I saw scorpions, snakes, vipers and lions.[25] Whenever they harmed me, I moistened the place [of the wound] with water and it healed.

Then, at the end of the desert, He opened up some gardens before me. I entered them and the water dried up. I stepped out of them and the water flowed again.[26]

Then I entered a darkness[27] and I was told, "Cast off your clothes[28] and throw away the water and the stones, for you have found [what you were looking for]." I discarded everything I had with me, without seeing where, and I remained [just as I am].

He said to me, "Now you are you."

Then He said to me, "Do you see how excellent this darkness is, how intense its brightness and how clear its light! This darkness is the place from which the lights rise,[29] the source from which the fountains of secrets spring forth and the [original] matter of the elements. From this darkness I have brought you into being, to it I make you return and I shall not remove you from it."

Then He showed me an opening like the eye of a needle. I went out towards it and I saw a beautiful radiance and a dazzling light.

He said to me, "Have you seen how intense is the darkness of this light? Stretch out your hand and you will not see it." I stretched it out and, indeed, I did not see it.

He said to me, "This is My light, in which none but Me can see himself."

Then He said to me, "Return to your darkness, for you are far from your kind."

"There is no one but you in this darkness[30] and I have brought into being from it no one but you;[31] from it I have taken you."

"I have created from light everything that exists except for you, who have been created from darkness."

"'They have not valued God as they ought.'[32] If He were in the light, then they would appreciate Him properly. You are truly My servant."[33]

"If you want to see Me, lift the veils from My face."

# *Notes*

1 An allusion to Q. 7: 172 (See Contemplation 1, n. 36). This Quranic verse refers to the "Lordly taking", when God, as Lord (*rabb*), took (*akhadha*) the descendants of Adam from the "back" of the children of Adam, and to the acknowledgement (*iqrār*) by the people taken by the Lord, that He is truly their Lord, expressed in their unanimous response when they said, "Yes, indeed!" We may note that in this Contemplation "the taking" (the act of taking hold) belongs to the Lord, while "the taken" (the one whom God takes hold of) always refers to the servant.

2 This refers to the taking by which "God removes the man from his servanthood (*'ubūdiyya*) bringing him towards Him by means of the attributes belonging to the lordly condition (*al-awṣāf al-rabbāniyya*) which He existentiates in him and [inversely] He removes from him the lordly attributes which He bestowed on him, to return him to his condition as servant. In this sense, for God, 'taking' is the same as 'letting go'." (IS)

3 "Not everything that is let go of is taken since if [God] had continued letting go without taking, [the servant] would not have replied 'Yes, indeed (*balā*)!'" (IS)

MS. B inverts the terms: "Not all that is taken is let go of . . .".

4 "Since you lean on Me [the Real]." (IS)

5 "Because I am not 'apprehended' by you." (IS)

6 According to Q. 7: 172, the divine taking occurs from behind (*ẓahr*: the back, from the same root as *ẓāhir*: manifest) which is the rear (and therefore hidden) side of man. (See Contemplation 1, n. 36.)

7 "That is, I manifested Myself through the 'coercive power' (*qahr*) by which I obliged you to acknowledge that I am your Lord, since if I had let go of you, you would not have acknowledged My Lordship and I would have remained hidden." (IS)

8 Namely, (1) taking the unified (*akhdh al-jam'*), (2) taking the differentiated (*farq*), and (3) taking the union of the unified (*jam' al-jam'*). (SA)

9 All taking (*akhdh*) which comes after the three kinds mentioned is no longer taking as such, but the vision of the essential reality of things.

10 Literally, "take".

11 The glorification of God by inanimate beings is mentioned in many Quranic passages (for example, those that refer to the glorification of all things (Q. 17: 44) or the praise of the mountains (Q. 21: 79), and the thunder (Q. 13: 13), and so on).

12 "That is, if I veiled you with coercive power (*qahr*), you would suffer from your condition of being compelled (*maqhūr*)." (IS)

13 An allusion to the creative word, or existentiating command, to which the following Quranic passage, among others, refers, "When He decrees a thing, He only says to it 'Be!' and it is." (Q. 2: 117)

14 MS. J repeats once more, "again I dispersed it and reunited it."

15 The Hand is the attribute of power since he saw the power that takes. (SA and IS)

16 "Absolute knowledge or omniscience (*al-ʿilm al-muṭlaq*)." (IS)

17 "That is, the situation was unclear to me for I could not distinguish the substance of the water [in which I was immersed]." (IS)

18 "The tablet (*lawḥ*) is the prescribed knowledge (*al-ʿilm al-mashrūʿ*)." (IS)

19 "This deserted place (*qafr*) is the knowledge of perplexity in the face of inability and limitation." (IS)

20 An allusion to a verse from the Sura of the Prophets which says, "We made from water every living thing." (Q. 21: 30)

21 "This green garden symbolizes the sayings of the Islamic tradition (*aḥādith al-sunna*)." (IS)

22 The names used to designate the flowers – whose lexical roots, in both cases, denote luminosity – refer more specifically to orange blossom (*azhār*) and anemones (*nuwwār*).

23 That is, let go of what you have obtained by means of your own ability. (SA)

24 "This desert (*ṣaḥrāʾ*) is the knowledge of transcendence (*tanzīh*) and the denudation which the knowledge of Unity involves (*tajrīd al-tawḥīd*)." (IS)

25 "The 'scorpions' and the 'serpents' symbolize misleading doubts." (IS)

26 "This refers to the garden of the verse 'There is nothing like Him' (Q. 42: 11), in which there is an implicit negation of the sciences. In such a garden nothing remains in your hand, which corresponds to the evaporation of the water." (IS) See also Contemplation 1, n. 12.

27 An expression referring to the darkness of the "Self" (the third person *huwa* implies absence and hiddenness) and the mutual correspondence which the Absolute Reality demands of servanthood. (IS)

28 "That is, divest yourself of yourself by abandoning pretension and remain in servanthood, for servanthood is the condition of man." (IS)

29 "The place from which the lights rise": *maṭlaʿ al-anwār*.

30 That is, there is no other gnostic (*ʿārif*) like you in your time. (SA)

31 This expression alludes to the singularity (*tafarrud*) of the gnostic, alone in his uniqueness (*aḥadiyya*). (SA)

32 Q. 6: 91 and 22: 74.

33 Because he is the perfect knower of God.

# 3

# Contemplation of the Light of the Veils (*sutūr*) as the Star of Strong Backing (*ta'yīd*) rises

IN THE NAME OF GOD,
THE COMPASSIONATE, THE MERCIFUL

The Real made me contemplate the light of the veils as the star of strong backing rose, and He said to me, "Do you know how many veils I have veiled you with?"

"No", I replied.

He said, "With seventy veils.[1] Even if you raise them you will not see Me,[2] and if you do not raise them you will not see Me."

"If you raise them you will see Me[3] and if you do not raise them you will see Me."[4]

"Take care of burning yourself!"[5]

"You are My sight,[6] so have faith. You are My Face, so veil yourself."[7]

Then He said to me, "Take all the veils away from Me. Reveal Me, for I have given you permission, keep me in the treasuries of the hidden, so that no other than Me sees Me, and invite the people to see Me. You will find behind each veil what the Beloved found.[8] So consider and recite [the verse ] 'Glory [to God] . . .' and when you come to [the words] '. . . the Hearer, the Seer',[9] understand well My intention and tell the servants what you have seen, so that you awaken their longing for Me and fill them with desire for Me, and you will be a mercy for them."[10]

Then He said to me, "Lift the veils one by one."

I lifted the first and I saw non-existence[11] [and I continued lifting, successively, the following veils]: existence, the existent, the [primordial] covenants, the return, the seas, the darknesses, yielding, instruction, derivation, permission, prohibition, transgression, anger, imprisonment, letters, generation, partial death, total death, direction, transmission, holding fast, the two feet, universal privilege, wrapping, splitting open, purification, recomposition, interdiction, sanctification, intercession, mounting, travelling,[12] milk,[13] knocking,[14] mixing, spirits, beauty, elevation, mastery, intimate conversation, dissolution, reaching the end,[15] letting go, love, removal of the intermediaries, the secret [centre] (*sirr*), the chests,[16] veracity,[17] irresistible power, sense of shame, boldness, leave-taking, inheritance, uprooting, annihilation, subsistence, jealousy, spiritual will,[18] unveiling, contemplation, majesty, beauty,[19] disappearance of the individual essence (*'ayn*), the imperceptible, the inaudible, the incomprehensible, the incommunicable, symbolic allusion, the whole.

A detailed explanation follows later.[20]

The servant[21] said: When I finished [lifting the veils] He asked me, "What have you seen?"

"Something magnificent", I replied.

Then He said to me, "What I have hidden from you is even more magnificent."[22]

"By My glory! I have not hidden anything from you, nor have I shown you anything."[23]

Then He burnt the veils [that remained] behind me,[24] and I saw the Throne.

He said to me, "Lift it."

So I lifted it and He said to me, "Throw it into the sea."[25]

I threw it and it disappeared. Then the sea cast it up again and He said to me, "Extract from the sea the Stone of Similarity."[26]

I extracted it and He said to me, "Lift up the Balance."[27] I lifted it up and He said to me, "Put the Throne and all it contains in one scale and put the Stone of Similarity in the other." The Stone weighed more. Then He said to me, "Even if you put in a million times the [weight of the] Throne up to the limit of what is possible,[28] this Stone would weigh more."

"And what is the name of this Stone?", I asked.

"Raise your head and look," He said. "You will find it written on all things."

I raised my head and I saw, indeed, that *alif*[29] was in everything. Then He covered me with fifty[30] veils and He uncovered from my face four hundred[31] veils so subtle that I never felt them.

Then He said to me, "Add what you have seen in all things to the veils. The result of this combination is the name of that Stone."[32]

"All this has been written since eternity without beginning, and all of it is [now] before you.[33] So read:

In the Name of God, the Compassionate, the Merciful

**[Letter] from the First Existence to the Second Existence:**[34]

Non-existence preceded you, you being already existent.[35] Then I made a covenant with you in the Presence of Oneness,[36] with your affirmation[37] that 'I am God and there is no divinity but Me'[38] and you gave Me testimony of that. Then I made you return.[39]

After that I brought you out[40] and I cast you into the sea.[41] Next I flung your parts into the darknesses,[42] then I sent you to them [as a messenger] and they accepted you with obedience and they yielded. I gave you the company and solace of a part of yourself,[43] whose company is licit for you.[44] Then I forbade you[45] My Presence, but I allowed you to enter it [against My wishes]. I became angry with you and I imprisoned you, even though you are blessed.

After this, I formed the letters[46] and I preserved them for you.[47] I gave you the Pen[48] and I sat you on your throne and you wrote on the Guarded Tablet[49] what I wanted of you. I vivified part of you,[50] giving you then the plenitude of life. Next I took out some parts of you,[51] I dispersed them in the corners of the prison [of the world], speaking in different kinds of languages. I fortified them[52] with [the gift of] impeccability and seated them on their chairs.

Then I singled out one of them,[53] for whose cause I have singled you out [too], and I strengthened him with the Words.[54] I purified him from all blemish, I forbade him to turn to created things, I sanctified his place[55] and I granted him the right of intercession in favour of all.

Then I plunged him into the sea and he mounted one of his mounts.[56] He journeyed by night in the instant[57] and I brought it down upon the Dome of Arīn.[58] Then I gave him total life and protected him from his partial nature,[59] and I addressed him from his centre,[60] saying, 'On leaving limitedness,[61] I will love you and on the departing of the spirits,[62] I will gladden you. Bring out and make manifest the heart of the veracious, and conquer. Take the secret of life and entrust it to whomsoever you wish. Draw the sword of vengeance: with it raise your sign and with it defeat whoever opposes you.

Then come to Me; let your son go, that he may take your place[63] and tell him to be consumed in annihilation by his subsistence, not to be jealous of [communicating] his revelation[64] and to contemplate Me in the attributes, but not in the essences,[65] because I am not contained by them.[66] Although he may listen, understand, know, allude, communicate, particularize or summarize, he will not comprehend Me. [However], in intuition (*shuʿūr*) things show themselves clearly to the people of vision.' "

# *Notes*

1 An allusion to the hadith (saying of the Prophet Muhammad) according to which God has seventy veils of light and "if these veils were removed, the glory of His face would burn up any creature who saw it." Muslim, *Īmān*, 293; Ibn Māja, *Muqaddima*, 13.

2 "Because by placing Me behind the veil you impose limits on Me." (IS)

3 "You will see Me in the theophany of non-existence (*maẓhar al-ʿadam*)." (IS)

4 "You will see Me in the existent places of manifestation (*maẓāhir al-mawjūdāt*)." (IS)

5 That is, "take care to raise the veil", according to Ibn Sawdakīn's commentary. This seems to be not only a warning of the danger in negative terms, but at the same time an invitation to persist in the intention to encounter this unveiling.

6 "That is, through you I see the things." (IS) According to Sitt al-ʿAjam, this refers to the revelation belonging to the Mosaic station to which the verse: ". . . so that you will be brought up in My sight" (Q. 20: 39) alludes, and also the Muhammadian station, expressed in the verse: ". . . for you are in Our eyes". (Q. 52: 48)

7 "That is, 'do not show your position in relation to Me to the people', for you are My face; an order which is similar to the words of God to the Prophet Muhammad, 'Say: I am only a human being (*bashar*) like you . . .' (Q. 18: 110), since by these words He hides him from the eyes of people so that they do not see his position as the face of the Real in the world." (IS)

8 That is, what Muhammad found during his night journey, on passing through the veils. See Ibn ʿArabī, *Kitāb al-Isrā'*, edited by S. Hakim.

"What is found behind each veil is not Me, but only a sign (*āya*) which indicates one of My places of manifestation. Otherwise, if you claim that something veils Me, you would limit Me . . . The Beloved (Muhammad) was taken on the night journey so that he could see some of the signs of his Lord, since night journeys are for the vision of signs." (IS)

9 See Q. 17: 1: "Glory to He who made His servant journey by night from the Holy Mosque to the Farthest Mosque, whose precincts we have blessed, in order to show him some of Our signs, for He is the

One who Hears and Sees!" According to tradition, this verse refers to Muhammad's night journey on the Burāq (heavenly steed, see below, n. 56) from the Mosque in Mecca to the Mosque in Jerusalem and his ascension through the seven heavens.

10 Following in the footsteps of Muhammad, who is told in the Quran: "We did not send you except as a mercy to the universes." (Q. 21: 107)

11 See Contemplation 1, nn. 3 and 5.

12 Travelling or following a road (*sulūk*) is crossing from one thing to another. (SA)

13 Milk (*laban*) is the symbol of knowledge. (SA) This symbolism refers to a well-known hadith, often quoted by Ibn ʿArabī, in which the Prophet recounts a dream and interprets milk as knowledge (*ʿilm*). See for example, Bukhārī, *ʿIlm*, 22, or Muslim, *Faḍā'il al-ṣaḥāba*, 16.

14 The knocking (*qarʿ*) means asking God to increase us in knowledge. (SA) An allusion to the verse: "Lord, increase me in knowledge!" (Q. 20: 114)

15 Reaching the end (*intihā'*) is reaching the intended goal. (SA)

16 The chests contain the certainty of the "secret [centre of the heart]" (*sirr*), since the chest is, in fact, the seat of the "secrets" (*asrār*), according to the saying of the Prophet: "Abū Bakr does not outdo you in fasting or in prayer but in something deposited in his chest." (SA)

17 The "confirmation of the truth" (*ṣiddīqiyya*) is the station of Abū Bakr, the Veracious (*al-Ṣiddīq*). See Contemplation 1, n. 23 and previous note.

18 *Himma* – the spiritual will or concentration of the heart – is the active energy or creativity which man can direct at will, as a means of producing an effect, or creating something whose maintenance depends on it. According to Ibn ʿArabī the best name to refer to it by is "divine providence" (*al-ʿināya al-ilāhiyya*). See S. Hakim, *al-Muʿjam al-ṣūfī*.

19 In all the MSS. the name "*al-jamāl*" (beauty) is mentioned again. It is possible that this repetition is due to an easy graphical error, where *jamāl* was written instead of *kamāl*, "perfection". *Kamāl* is the synthesis of *jamāl*, "beauty" and *jalāl*, "majesty".

20 Further on in this contemplation, he recounts in sequential form the process of the unveiling of the seventy veils. See Appendix 4 for further explanation of the veils and correspondences between them.

21 For the first time in the text, the term *ʿabd*, "servant", is used to refer to the contemplative who is talking with God. See Contemplation 1, n. 4 and 14, n. 17.

22 "I have hidden from you the knowledge of Me through Myself, and this knowledge is more sublime than all that you have seen." (IS)

23 "I did not hide any of the possibilities (*mumkināt*) from you, nor did I show you anything of what you are seeking, which is the Real (*al-ḥaqq*)." (IS)

24 "He made me leave the veils behind." (IS)

25 "The sea of knowledge (*ʿilm*)." (IS)

26 The Stone of Similarity (*ḥajar al-mithl*), an allusion to Q. 42: 11, refers to the Perfect Man (*al-insān al-kāmil*). (IS) See also Contemplation 1, n. 12.

27 The Balance is the symbol of justice (*ʿadl*). The act of raising it up indicates that the Perfect Man, after this, takes Justice upon himself, without preference. (SA)

28 A theoretical numerical limit.

29 The *alif* is the first letter of the Arabic alphabet, although for Ibn ʿArabī it is not a question of a letter (*ḥarf*) as such. The *alif* is the underlying principle of all the letters, where it lies hidden, contained in their names and graphical forms. In fact, all the names of the letters include an *alif*, either explicitly in the name: for example, *wāw* (written *wāw–alif–wāw*); or implicitly, in the name of one of the letters of its name: for example, *nūn* (written *nūn–wāw–nūn*). Moreover the *alif*, a vertical line, is symbolically the original form of the letter that gives rise to the others and the substance with which the letters are modelled. The *alif* is not confined to any specific degree and therefore it is the symbol by which one alludes to the unconditioned Essence. See Contemplation 5, nn. 8 and 9. See S. Hakim, *al-Muʿjam al-ṣūfī*.

30 Numerical value of the letter *nūn*.

31 Numerical value of the letter *tāʾ*.

32 By joining together the *alif–nūn–tāʾ*, the pronoun *anta*, "you" (singular) is formed. The graphic representation of the letter *tāʾ*, which is numerically equivalent to four hundred, contains two dots which allude to duality. By omitting the *tāʾ* of the four hundred veils, the *alif* "written on everything" and the *nūn* of fifty veils, which is written with a single diacritical point, remain. The graphic union

of both letters represents the pronoun for the first person singular *anā*, "I", an allusion to the divine I and probably (according to this interpretation), to the encoded name of the Stone.

33 Literally, "between your hands".

34 This is the detailed explanation announced after the enumeration of the seventy veils. See n. 20 above.

35 "That is, it preceded you as 'you', since you were already existent due to My knowledge (*li-ʿilmī*) [potentially, implicitly] but not in My knowledge (*fī-ʿilmī*) [actually, explicitly]." (IS)

36 Presence of Oneness: *ḥaḍrat al-waḥdāniyya*; MS. B has *tawḥīd*.

37 This is another allusion to the covenant referred to in Q. 7: 172. See Contemplation 1, n. 36.

38 Q. 20: 14.

39 "That is, I made you return to the hiddenness (*ghayba*) which follows the covenant." (IS)

40 "That is, I made you come out of the hiddenness towards unlimited Nature." (IS)

41 "That is, into knowledge (*ʿilm*)." (IS)

42 Limited nature.

43 The address is directed towards the Intellect, to whom He gave the company of the Soul (*nafs*). Just as God created Eve for Adam, so He created the Universal Soul for the Universal Intellect. (IS)

44 That is, He gave him permission so that he should know by this licence the meaning of freedom. (IS)

45 He forbids the servant so that by this prohibition he may know the measure of servanthood. (IS)

46 An allusion to the marriage (of the Soul and the Intellect), the coupling (the third factor or link), and general procreation (*tawālud*). (IS)

47 So that you would know their realities and distinguish the various degrees. (IS)

48 "Giving the Pen" means granting power over generating meanings, because the pen in reality is the creator of the letters which indicate meanings. The form of the gift implies the transference of creative power as an attribute. (SA)

It is worth bearing in mind the Quranic passage which states that "God taught Adam all the names". (Q. 2: 31) Adam's knowledge of the names is what enables human beings to generate meanings.

49 "The Guarded Tablet is the place where the Pen generates the

manifest form and where the beings are created according to the Divine Will." (SA)

50 The place which receives the Divine Knowledge. (IS)

51 He is referring to the messengers.

52 The word that is translated here as "fortified" comes from the same root as "strong backing" (*ta'yīd*), which appears in the title of this contemplation. The root also contains the following meanings: support, assistance, confirmation, protection, rendering victorious and favour. Note the repetition in the following sentence of the text: "I *strengthened* him with the Words." Ibn ʿArabī also uses the word *ta'yīd* in the epilogue: "When the High God wishes to grant His servants some of these [special] knowledges, He disposes the mirror of his heart towards success, looks at it with the eye of benevolence and help (*tawfīq*) and supports it with the sea of strong backing (*ta'yīd*)." See Appendix 3.

53 He is referring to Muhammad.

54 That is, the words of the Quran.

55 "He means that no other will have access to it [literally, 'will tread on it'] in the same way, since it is the place where only he may ascend, for it is the place of the two feet between the Throne and the Pedestal." (SA)

56 An allusion to the Burāq, whose name comes from the same root as "lightning" (*barq*), and which, according to tradition, served as a mount to Muhammad on his night journey and on his heavenly ascension to the Throne.

57 In the instant (*al-ān*), now, the *present* and indivisible time of the state. The whole night journey and ascension of the Prophet is said to have taken place within a single instant.

58 The point of equilibrium (*iʿtidāl*) which, since it does not incline towards any direction, maintains and preserves this human constitution (IS). Arīn is a place which is equidistant from the four cardinal points and therefore represents the centre of the world, according to Islamic cosmography. See Contemplation 8, n. 22, and also M. Chodkiewicz, *An Ocean without Shore*, p. 79. Here, the Dome of Arīn may refer to the Dome of the Rock, from which the Prophet's ascension through the heavens took place.

59 That is, from the physical world of nature. (IS)

60 That is, from the "point of equilibrium" (*maḥall al-iʿtidāl*). (IS)

61 This means extinction (*fanā'*) or death before dying.

62 This refers to natural death. At the moment when the spirit of the gnostic departs from the physical body, God (*al-ḥaqq*) reveals to him the promised happiness. (SA)

63 That is, let him succeed you in the function of heir and in (the actualization of) similarity. (SA)

64 That is, may he not hesitate to reveal his knowledge, since only people endowed with comprehension (literally, "his people") will grasp it. (SA)

65 Because to contemplate God in the essences of created things would imply the doctrine of "incarnation" (*ḥulūl*): the indwelling of one essence within another – that the Divine Essence is somehow localized in a created thing. (SA)

66 Literally, "My individual essence (*'aynī*) disappears from them."

# 4

# Contemplation of the Light of Intuition (*shuʿūr*) as the Star of Transcendence (*tanzīh*) rises

IN THE NAME OF GOD,
THE COMPASSIONATE, THE MERCIFUL

The Real made me contemplate the light of intuition[1] as the star of transcendence rose, and He said to me, "I hide Myself in evidence[2] and intuition[3] from the people of veils."[4]

Then He said to me, "Poetry is confined and it is the place of symbol and enigma. If they knew[5] that the symbol and enigma of things is in the intensity of clarity, they would follow that.[6] The luminous verses of the Quran have been revealed as indications of meanings which [otherwise] would never be understood."

"See Me in the sun[7] and look for Me in the moon,[8] but avoid Me in the stars."[9]

"Do not be like the bird of Jesus."[10]

"Look for Me in the vicegerent and amongst the guardians of the night[11] and you will find Me."

Then He said to me, "When you see the cattle, horses and donkeys immersed in water up to their necks, then ride the mules,[12] and leaning on the walls,[13] try to reach the bank.[14] If an obstacle should arise cutting you off from the bank, cover your eyes with your hands[15] and let your hair[16] fall over your forehead[17] and enter the stream [without fear], for the water will not reach your saddlebow[18] and you will be safe. Whoever is riding a horse or a donkey will perish in the river, but not he who is riding a mule."[19]

Then He said to me, "If you stay in intuition, you will be the middle degree.[20] Whoever is beneath you will look towards you and whoever is above you, will turn towards you, so that there is no one above you.[21] In intuition you will find the instant."

"If you are the middle degree then travel in spring!"[22]

Then He said to me, "Light is a veil and darkness is a veil. In the line between them both you will be aware of what is most beneficial. So follow this line[23] closely, and if you arrive at the point in which it originates, make it disappear in the sunset prayer.[24] Then sleep after the odd prayer of the night.[25] When dawn comes, the legal obligation will be lifted,[26] the burden [of prescriptions] will fall away, and you will be you, beyond such attributions."[27]

"If the Command [of God] descends, do not give up,[28] because if you give up, you will perish."

"If you ride on the mule, do not look at which side you are on, for you will die. If you ride, stay silent."

# *Notes*

1 "Mystical intuition (*shuʿūr*) is the integrating, synthetic knowledge (*ʿilm al-ijmāl*)." (IS) This word, which has the same root (*sh–ʿ–r*) as "poetry" (*shiʿr*) and "hair" (*shaʿr*), here means the "intuitive knowledge", "profound and immediate awareness" or "interior perception" which one has of something.

2 That is, "I hide in evidence (*bayān*)" by the very clarity and intensity of manifestation. (IS)

3 A double allusion to prose and poetry, the explicit and the implicit, analysis and synthesis.

4 The people of veils (*ahl al-sutūr*) are those whose knowledge is founded only on a superficial reading of books and signs.

5 That is, if "the people of veils" knew.

6 That is, the way of clarity.

7 "That is, in the plain and obvious meanings in which there is no doubt . . . in certainty and perfect clarity." (IS)

8 "That is, look for Me in the places of manifestation, since in this way you will only find yourself." (IS)

9 "That is, in the Names (*al-asmāʾ*)." (IS)

10 "Do not stay with the [secondary] cause (*sabab*) which gave you existence, even if it is immediately perceptible; rather, be with the one who gave you existence in reality, which is God." (IS)

An allusion to the bird mentioned in the verse: "I shall create for you, from clay, something resembling a bird. Then I will blow on it and it will become a bird, by permission of God." (Q. 3:49)

11 The *khalīfa* ("vicegerent" or "representative" of God) holds the highest rank in the spiritual hierarchy, whilst the "nightwatchmen" (*al-ʿasas*) hold the lowest rank. (IS) According to Sitt al-ʿAjam, the term *khalīfa* refers to the Envoy (the Prophet Muhammad) and the term *ʿasas*, "nightwatchmen", refers to the guardians who watch over the religion, to the *awliyāʾ*, the saints and friends of God, the gnostics who ask help from the station of the messengers and who, in their turn, help others. (SA)

12 The mule (*baghl*) is a cross between a horse and a donkey, and so a *barzakh*, "isthmus", or intermediary between two orders. This symbol implies that the contemplative is not restricted to a limited form (in one order), but adopts a form which unites two or more

aspects, since if he oriented himself exclusively towards one of them he would lose the perspective of the other. (IS)

In his summary of the life of the Prophet, Ibn ʿArabī informs us that the Prophet had a mule called Duldul (see *Ihtiṣār sīrat rasūl Allāh*, ed. Muhammad Kamāl al-Dīn ʿIzz al-Dīn, Beirut, 1987, p. 102). See also *K. Ayyām al-sha'n*, p. 4, where Ibn ʿArabī refers to the Prophet riding a mule.

13 The wall is what you lean on, whether it is a power attributed to you or divine support. (IS)

14 "The bank [firm, level ground] is where your knowledge resides." (IS)

15 "That is, stop your imagination and speculative faculties." (IS) The word "imagination"(*khayāl*) is from the same root as *khayl*, "horse". Also, speculation is indirectly associated with the donkey in the Quranic image of the "donkey carrying books". (Q. 62: 5)

16 The term *shaʿr*, "hair", from the same root as *shuʿūr*, "intuitive knowledge", alludes to interior vision. See above, n. 1.

17 "That is, apply your 'synthetic intuitive knowledge' (*shuʿūr*) to the centre of your awareness to see what it brings you. If you do this, you will leave the station of imagination (*maqām al-khayāl*), you will reach the river [*nahr*, from the same root as *nahār*, 'day', 'daylight'] and you will be saved, whilst those who ride horses or donkeys – having restricted Reality (*al-ḥaqq*) to a particular order – will perish, since God, glory to Him, is not limited." (IS)

18 Literally, "the saddlebow of your saddle". The word *sarj*, "saddle", comes from the same root as *sirāj*, "lamp". See Contemplation 9, n. 22.

19 The donkey, carrying theoretical knowledge, is an allusion to those who postulate the doctrine of absolute transcendence (such as the Muʿtazilites). The horse of the "imagination" is an allusion to those who postulate the doctrine of absolute immanence (such as the anthropomorphists and pantheists), whilst the mule represents those who adopt an intermediate way, the union of the opposites, reconciling the incomparability (*tanzīh*) and the similarity (*tashbīh*) of God, which are complementary aspects of knowledge.

20 The intermediate degree between intelligible meanings and physical things. (IS)

21 "Since you are the union of the two extremes." (IS)

22 "Spring (*al-rabīʿ*) [from the same root as *arbaʿa*, 'four'] is an allusion

to temporality or the advent of time which is the first principle of manifestation." (IS)

23 "Light veils darkness and vice versa. The line between them unites them, because it has a side facing towards light and a side facing darkness. Therefore, be the confluence of the essential realities." (IS)

24 At dusk, which is the line or "isthmus" between night and day, the sunset prayer (*ṣalāt al-maghrib*) is performed. It is the fourth obligatory prayer which consists of an odd number of *rakaʿāt* (sequences of movements and ritual postures). See Contemplation 12, n. 8.

25 This oddness reflects the singleness of God. The sunset prayer belongs to the day, whereas there is another odd prayer (*witr* or *watr*) in the night which is a supererogatory prayer. See Contemplation 12, n. 10.

26 "That is, the legal obligation (*taklīf*) will cease insofar as it is an imposition, and so it will no longer be a burden, although the performing of the prescribed works will continue [as is suitable to servanthood]." (IS)

27 "That is, beyond attributing a troublesome or formal character to the ritual action, but performing it in such a way that it is a joy and loving intimacy with God." (IS)

28 "That is, receive the orders of the law with steadiness." (IS)

# 5

# Contemplation of the Light of Silence (*ṣamt*) as the Star of Negation (*salb*) rises

IN THE NAME OF GOD,
THE COMPASSIONATE, THE MERCIFUL

The Real made me contemplate the light of silence as the star of negation[1] rose, and He made me speechless. [However], there did not remain a single place in the whole universe where my word was not inscribed, nor was there any writing which did not come from my substance[2] and my dictation.

Then He said to me, "Silence is your essential reality."

"Silence is nothing other than you, although it does not belong to you."

"If you made 'the silent'[3] your object of worship, you would be following those who worshipped the calf[4] and you would be amongst the worshippers of the sun and the moon.[5] But if 'the silent' is not the object of your worship, then you are Mine and not its [servant]."

Then He said to me, "I created you with speech which is the essential reality of your silence, so that, although you speak, you are silent."

"Through you I speak, through you I give, through you I take, through you I expand,[6] through you I contract, through you I see, through you I give existence and through you I am known."

"For you I speak, for you I give, for you I take, for you I expand and for you I contract, for you I am visible, for you I am given existence and for you I am made known."

Then He said to me, "You are the place of My seeing and you are My attribute.[7] So do not speak except when I look at you. I look at you constantly, so address the people continuously but do not speak."

"My silence is the exterior of your existence and your being."

"If I had remained silent, *you* would not exist; if *you* had spoken, I would not have been known. Speak, then, so that I may be known."

Then He said to me, "The *alif* is silent[8] whilst the letters speak. The *alif* articulates the letters, but the letters do not articulate the *alif*.[9] The letters are regulated by the *alif* and the *alif* accompanies them always, without their realizing."

"The letters are Moses[10] and the *alif* is the staff."[11]

Then He said to me, "Your existence is in silence and your non-existence in articulation."

"Whoever is silent is not silent; rather, whoever is not silent is silent."

"Whether you speak or are silent you are speaking,[12] and even if you spoke for evermore through all eternity, you would remain in silence."

"If you remain silent, everything will be guided by you and if you speak, everything will go astray through you. Rise beyond and you will discover."

## *Notes*

1 "Silence (*ṣamt*) is a negative attribute." (IS)

2 *Mādda*, "matter", is from the same root as *midād*, "ink".

3 "The silent" (*al-ṣāmit*) is that which is not endowed with speech. This is an allusion to the idols and their inability to reply.

4 An allusion to the people of Moses who worshipped the golden calf when Moses hurried away to meet his Lord. "The people of Moses made from their trinkets, in his absence, the image of a calf which lowed." (Q. 7: 148)

5 In alchemical symbolism, the sun corresponds to gold and the moon to silver. The people of the sun and the moon are, in this sense, those whose objects of worship are gold and silver, that is, transient accidents and everything that is not God. (IS)

6 "Through you I expand" is omitted from the Manisa manuscript but is included in MSS. B and J.

7 That is "My sight", one of the seven attributes of the divinity. See Contemplation 9, n. 29.

8 "This means that the *alif* is not one of the articulated or voiced letters." (IS) See Contemplation 3, n. 29.

9 The *alif* is implicitly present in all the letters, since the letters, when they are pronounced, are a discontinuous flow of air, whilst the *alif* is a continuous flow, without any determined limit. One could say that by articulating the *alif* (the flow of expired air) at the points of articulation, thereby segmenting it, the various letters are manifested. (IS) See Contemplation 11, n. 1.

10 That is, the letters are articulated. Moses represents the articulation of speech, since in the Quran he is called *kalīm Allāh*, "the one who speaks with God". See Q. 4: 164; also Exodus 34: 5.

11 That is, the *alif* is not pronounced. According to Ibn ʿArabī, the staff symbolizes silence because it is "silent". In spite of its silence, the Divine Miracle was manifested in the staff of Moses. Similarly, the sign/verse (*āya*) is in the *alif*, not in the letters, since only God can produce an effect. (IS) See Q. 2: 60.

12 "Due to the manifestation of the meanings which arise from you." (IS)

# 6

# Contemplation of the Light of Elevation (*maṭlaʿ*) as the Star of Unveiling (*kashf*) rises

IN THE NAME OF GOD,
THE COMPASSIONATE, THE MERCIFUL

The Real made me contemplate the light of elevation[1] as the star of unveiling rose, and He said to me, "You have ascended from the limit and yet you have not separated from it, for if it were not for the exterior, the interior would not be known;[2] if it were not for the limit, the Watchtower of Elevation would not be witnessed. The rising of the light is witnessed by darkness, and the rising of the full moon is witnessed by the sun."

"From the Watchtower, whoever descends descends[3] and whoever ascends ascends.[4] Beware of Me in the Watchtower! If I see that the exterior of your wall exceeds the limit, I will make you descend from the Watchtower to the exterior;[5] however, if you stay within the limit,[6] the Watchtower will want you to stay in your position."[7]

Then He said to me:[8]

- "Glory rises in Closeness and the magnificence of the world bears witness to it.
- The Instant rises in time-suspension[9] and the sea of Compassionate Beatitude bears witness to it.

- The proper attitude [required by] the knowledges[10] rises and the correct attribution of actions bears witness to it, recalling the warning at the Watchtower.
- The Watchtower of Elevation rises and the limit bears witness to it.
- Death rises and the power of predestination bears witness to it.
- Gentleness rises in the mansion of modesty and the appearance of speech bears witness to it.
- The name[11] rises and the veil bears witness to it.
- Release rises and vision bears witness to it.[12]
- The eye of internal vision rises and unveiling bears witness to it.
- Supplication rises and distance[13] bears witness to it.
- Forgiveness rises and transgression bears witness to it.
- What is not unveiled rises and sainthood bears witness to it.
- What is above the Throne rises and the indication of the Real bears witness to it.
- The Sea of Return rises and loss of light[14] bears witness to it.
- Indigence rises and the manifestation of I-ness[15] bears witness to it.
- Grandeur rises and Hidden Identity[16] bears witness to it.
- Straying rises and whatness bears witness to it.[17]
- The veil rises and whyness[18] bears witness to it.
- The clothing rises and quantity[19] bears witness to it.
- Oneness rises and non-existence bears witness to it.
- Free will rises and the [primordial] covenant bears witness to it.[20]
- What is before him rises and the spiritual abodes bear witness to it.
- Quietude rises and establishment bears witness to it.
- The heart[21] rises and observation bears witness to it.
- Knowledge of the covenant rises and good form bears witness to it.
- The speaking night rises and amazement bears witness to it.
- Servanthood rises and staying[22] [in this station] bears witness to it.

- The letters rise and expressions bear witness to them.
- Strength rises and drawing near bears witness to it.
- Trembling rises and worship bears witness to it.
- The perception of veracity[23] rises and prostrate submission bears witness to it."

When I saw both risings and testimonies succeeding one another uninterruptedly, I asked, "Will there be an end to all this?"

He said, "Not whilst eternity lasts."

Then He said to me, "All that you have beheld and all that was hidden from you and which will occur to you unexpectedly, all that is for you, because of you, and is in you. But had I revealed the least of the secrets of the mystery of the essential Unity of Divinity which I deposited in you, you would not have been capable of bearing its weight and you would have been consumed by fire. What would become of you then, if I were to reveal to you something of Myself or of My essential attributes!"

"Persist for all eternity and you will see nothing but yourself in every station. Quicker than the blinking of an eye you will ascend through stations you have never glimpsed and to which you will never return, but they will remain in you without surpassing your capacity."

"If you could evaluate your worth you would limit yourself and, in reality, you have no limits; so how could your worth be evaluated? Since you are incapable of appreciating your own worth – which is proper – follow good form and do not seek to know My worth, for you could never succeed in evaluating it, even if you were the most noble being in My [eternal] knowledge."

Then He said to me, "Know that every day seventy thousand mysteries from My Majesty pass through the heart of the gnostic never to return. If just one of those mysteries were revealed to someone who has not reached this station, it would consume him."[24]

"If it were not for you, the spiritual stations would not have been manifested, nor would the order of the spiritual abodes have been established; the mysteries would not exist, the lights would not shine nor would there be darkness; there would be no rising, nor limit, nor exterior nor interior,[25] nor first nor last. You are My Names and the indication of My Essence, for your essence is My essence and your attributes are My attributes."[26]

Then He said to me, "So appear in My existence on My behalf in order to speak to them with My tongue without them realizing it. They will see you talking, although [really] you are silent. They will see you moving although you are still. They will see you as the knower although you are the known. They will see you as powerful, although power is exercised over you. Whoever sees you, has seen Me. Whoever honours you, has honoured Me. Whoever insults you, has insulted himself. Whoever degrades you, has only degraded himself. You punish whom you wish[27] and you reward whom you wish, without any will of your own."

"You are My mirror, My house, My dwelling-place, My hidden treasure and the seat of My knowledge. If it were not for you, I would not be known or worshipped, I would not be thanked or denied."

"If I want to punish someone, he will deny you. If I want to grace him, he will show gratitude towards you. Praise to you, may you be exalted! You are the praised, the glorified, the magnified. The goal of learning and knowledge is to be attached to you."

"I have brought into being in you the attributes and qualities[28] by which I want you to know Me."

"The limit of your knowledge depends on the capacity I have given you; therefore you only know yourself."

Then He said to me, "I alone possess the attributes of Majesty and Beauty: no one other than Me knows them. If anyone had knowledge of My knowledge, My will and the totality of My attributes – which can neither be summed up nor defined – I would be neither God nor Creator."

"Every declaration of transcendence with which you proclaim My incomparability refers to you, since only the one to whom it is possible to impute shortcomings can be removed from them and sanctified from them. However, I am completely transcendent in Myself, for Myself and through Myself, incomprehensible and imperceptible."

"The looks fall short, the intellects are perplexed, the hearts blind, the knowers lost in a desert of bewilderment, and the understandings, plunged into stupefaction, are incapable of grasping the least secret of the revelation of My Grandeur. How then could they encompass it? Your knowledge is scattered dust. Your qualities are nothing. Your reality is only a metaphor in a corner of My being."

Then He said to me, "Come back, for you cannot go beyond your rank. All of you are ignorant of Me, dumb, blind, incapable, inadequate, speechless, bewildered. You have absolutely nothing whatsoever, however paltry it may be, that belongs to you."[29]

"If I gave power over all of you to the most insignificant of creeping animals from among My creatures and the weakest of My army, it would annihilate, destroy and utterly demolish you. So how do you claim and maintain that you are Me and I am you. You have claimed the impossible and you are living in error. You have split into factions and become dispersed, 'each group is happy with what it has',[30] but the Truth is beyond all that."

"O My servant and place of My vision in My creation! Communicate about Me truthfully, for I am the Veracious One."

Then He said to me, "By My Glory and My Majesty and by what I have hidden of My resplendent knowledge, I shall punish, as I have never punished anyone in any world, whoever denies My messengers and denies My special favour to them from among the rest of the servants; and denies My attributes claiming that I have no attributes, and imposes conditions on Me and confines Me; and denies My Word and interprets it without any knowledge of it; and denies the fact that he will meet Me, saying that I have not created him and that I am not capable of resurrecting him as I originally created him; and denies the gathering [of the Day of Judgement] and the resurrection, and does not believe in the [reality] of the pool of the Prophet,[31] or in My Balance and My Straight Path, or that he has to see Me, or in My Fire and My Garden, maintaining that these are [only allegorical] images and [symbolic] expressions whose meaning goes beyond the apparent."

"By My Power and My Majesty! They will be returned, and then they will know who has followed the straight path and who has been guided. We shall take revenge on those [who denied] in the abode of shame and torment as I informed them in My books."

"They denied Me and sanctioned their passions. They let themselves be seduced by vanities, and their demons played with them. 'You and what you serve besides God will be fuel for Hell to which you will come.'"[32]

"Stay within My limit and meditate on My book, for it is the radiant light, which contains the hidden secret of My truth. My path stretches over My fire, so woe betide whoever denies Me!"

Then He said to me, "O My servant! Have I veiled your heart from Me and from My knowledge and from acting freely in My kingdom and My angelic realm, [veiling you] in your world through the persisting of your body and your [need for] nourishment and your ability to act freely with people of your kind? Do you not know that the gnostics as they are today, will be like that tomorrow, with their bodies in the gardens of paradise and their hearts in the presence of the Compassionate? 'Every group is happy with what it has' and each has a known drink. They will be returned and then they will know. It is as if they have not heard 'the day the leg will be revealed and they will be summoned to prostrate . . .'."[33]

# Notes

1 The *maṭla'* (or it can also be read as *muṭṭala'*) refers to everything which the servant comes to know through mystical intuition or unveiling (*kashf*) without having tasted or experienced it himself (*dhawq*) and without it corresponding to his state, since if such knowledge was due to his state, it would not be *maṭla'*. By this means, the saint reveals the stations of the prophets and this is the contemplation called *maṭla'*. (IS)

The term *maṭla'*, the name of the place having the root *ṭ–l–'*, has, among others, the following meanings: dawn, sunrise, point of departure, point of ascent, elevation, ladder, lookout, watchtower. It also refers to the spiritual station of the Day of Resurrection and may be understood as mystical perception occurring in an elevated state of consciousness.

The term comes from a saying of the Prophet: "No verse of the Quran has come down without it having an exterior [meaning] and an interior [meaning] and in every letter there is a limit (*ḥadd*) and in every limit there is a place of ascension (*muṭṭala'*)." Ibn 'Arabī mentions the four corresponding human types: "the people of the exterior" (*rijāl al-ẓāhir*), "the people of the interior" (*rijāl al-bāṭin*), "the people of the limit" (*rijāl al-ḥadd*), and "the people of elevation" (*rijāl al-maṭla'*). He also tells us that one of his teachers, one of the greatest shaykhs he met, al-Shakkaz of Priego, related these four categories of people to those referred to in the Quran respectively as: those who "are true to their covenant with God" (Q. 33:23); those "whom neither trade nor business distract from the remembrance of God" (Q. 24:37); those of "the battlements [heights, between heaven and hell] who know everyone by their marks" (Q. 7:46); and those who come to God "on foot" when He calls to them (Q. 22:27). See also R. W. J. Austin, *Sufis of Andalusia*, pp. 111–12, C. Addas, *Quest for the Red Sulphur*, p. 171, and W. C. Chittick, *The Self-Disclosure of God*, p. 219.

The opposition of the terms *ḥadd* and *maṭla'* (or *muṭṭala'*) may be represented graphically by the image of a wall (limitation, definition, divine law), from which a watchtower representing mystical elevation, symbolic allusion and inspired intuition rises up and which, supported by the wall, allows the surveyance of the ocean of revelation beyond its limits. In Ibn ʿArabī's time, the watchtower would have been a familiar sight.

Ibn ʿArabī devoted an independent treatise to these terms, the *K. al-Ḥadd wa-l-muṭṭalaʿ* (see R.G. 207), which has not yet been found.

2 Because things are known by their opposite. (IS)

3 That is, on contemplating the elevation, whoever presumptuously lays claim (to the divinity) alleges: "I am the Truth (*anā 'l-ḥaqq*)." (IS)

4 "That is, he knows his [ontological] limitation, stays within his limits and is saved [from pretension by recognizing his condition of servanthood]." (IS)

5 "That is, I will make you descend [from the elevation of mystical perception] to the first degree which is the 'exterior part' or 'literal meaning' (*ẓahr*)." (IS)

6 That is, if you stay with the knowledge of your rank and capacity. (IS)

7 You will be sought, not seeking, and the elevation will descend to make your acquaintance. (IS)

8 There follows a series of thirty-one sentences in which the same structure is repeated: "X rises (*ṭalaʿa*) and Y bears witness to it (*shahida lahu*)", that is, when something is manifested or made known (in the *maṭlaʿ*), something else testifies to that revelation (in the *mashhad*).

The thirty-one sentences have a symbolic correspondence with the consonants of the Arabic alphabet and the vowels. The Arabic language uses thirty-one segmental phonemes, of which twenty-eight are consonants and three are vowels.

9 The expression "pause" or "suspension" (of time) (*waqfa*) refers to a present condition (an indivisible period of time) which is neither past nor future (nor an interval between the two), a state in which temporality remains still. (IS)

10 Truth (*al-ḥaqq*) is only made known to those whose conduct is impeccable (*al-udabāʾ*). The gnostic combines two sorts of tact or good form (*adab*): the good form, or proper attitude, required to find knowledge and the good form bestowed by knowledge. (IS)

11 The "name" is only used in the absence of the named. If it were not for this absence, we would use "you", but when the second person is absent, we need to use their name. When we call someone who is

present by their name, it is an expression of acknowledgement, not of denomination in the strict sense. (IS)

12 "That is, true release or freedom [from attachment to blameworthy things] only takes place through vision. If you see it you know from what you are released, but if you do not see it you cannot be safe from returning to it after being released (*al-tabarrī*)." (IS)

13 "Supplication is a call from the peak of distance." (IS) This comment by Ibn Sawdakīn refers to a famous saying by Ibn al-ʿArīf, quoted by Ibn ʿArabī in the *Futūḥāt*: "The 'allusion' (*ishāra*) is a call from the peak of distance." See Ibn al-ʿArīf, *Maḥāsin al-majālis*, edited by M. Asín Palacios, p. 76.

14 "When they are bereft of light they return, according to God's Word, 'It will be said, "Turn back, then seek a light!"(Q. 57: 13)'" (IS)

15 The I-ness (*aniyya* or *inniyya*) is the "individual being", which Ibn ʿArabī defines as "the reality by way of relationship (*al-ḥaqīqa bi-ṭarīq al-iḍāfa*)". See *al-Futūḥāt al-Makkiyya* (edited by O. Yahia), vol. XIII, p. 182. See also Contemplation 10, n. 5. On the derivation of the term *aniyya* from *anā* (I), see Arberry's commentary on *Mawqif* 49, l. 7, in Niffarī, *Mawāqif and Mukhāṭabāt*, p. 233.

16 This term is also translated as He-ness or it-ness. (See W. C. Chittick, *The Sufi Path of Knowledge*, p. 394, n. 15.) Ibn ʿArabī defines the term *huwiyya* – derived from the pronoun *huwa* meaning "he" or "it" – as "the hidden essential reality (*al-ḥaqīqat al-ghaybiyya*)". (*Futūḥāt*, p. 183)

17 "That is, since the quiddity [what-it-is-ness] of the Real (*māhiyyat al-ḥaqq*) is unknown, the creature is lost in it." (IS)

18 The term *limayya* ("whyness"), suggesting reason, purpose or cause, is derived from *limā* ("why?").

19 The philosophical term *kammiyya*, which is derived from *kamm*, means "quantity" or "multiplicity".

20 By "free will", he means the commandment of God, and by "the covenant bears witness to it" he means the fact that God makes a covenant by which He will reward the servant in accordance with what He imposes on him. (IS)

21 The term *qalb*, "heart", can also mean "transformation" (*taḥwīl*).

22 "That is, to remain [in obedience to] the command and [to avoid] the prohibition." (IS)

23 See Contemplations 1, n. 23, 3, nn. 16 and 17, and 10, n. 9.

24 When commenting on this, Ibn ʿArabī explained to Ibn Sawdakīn that "God has a special kingdom set aside for mysteries or secrets, from which the spirits of the letters are breathed into the whole world. The Divine Word '. . . and I have breathed into him of My spirit' (Q. 15:29) contains seventy thousand powers, so that the heart of the gnostic receives seventy thousand secrets every day: each power confers a secret and each secret bestows one of the knowledges of divinity, and this each of the days of the world." (IS)

25 This is another reference to the hadith mentioned in note 1 above.

26 Since in reality there is no other essence apart from the Divine Essence and all beings are names which refer to It.

27 "That is, the punishment prescribed by the Law." (IS)

28 Intrinsic and extrinsic attributes, respectively.

29 Literally, "neither a pellicle, nor a filament, nor even a tiny spot on the back of a date-stone".

30 Q. 23:53.

31 The pool (*ḥawḍ*) from which he will give drink to the believers in the life to come.

32 Q. 21:98.

33 "The day when the leg will be revealed and they will be summoned to prostrate, but they will not be able." (Q. 68:42)

# 7

# Contemplation of the Light of the Leg (*sāq*) as the Star of the Summons (*duʿāʾ*) rises

IN THE NAME OF GOD,
THE COMPASSIONATE, THE MERCIFUL

The Real made me contemplate the light of the Leg[1] as the star of the summons[2] rose, and He said to me, "Rely on it,[3] for it is the irrevocable Order which issues from the Presence of Majesty in whose dominion it manifests. Beware when it appears!"

"If you hold onto it [with strength], I shall speak to you,[4] and the Beloved[5] will find you in My company."

Then He said to me, "Do not hold onto the Leg except when the sky folds in and sways from side to side, the mountains start to move and the two feet depart, and everything dead vanishes and only the living remains."

"If the Leg appears [to you], beware of negation."[6]

"We distracted them[7] from seeing the Leg, when they were crossing the limit, by keeping them occupied with [the idea of] the happiness to come."

"Upon the Leg stands the evident proof and honour is due to it, even though it is subordinate."[8]

"When [the Leg] appears the splendour of the sun[9] is intensified and the moon[10] vanishes and the stars[11] fall and scatter and [everything] returns to Him."

Then He said to me, "Amongst My servants are those who occupy themselves with the Divine Pen, leaving aside the Leg; those who occupy themselves with the heart, leaving aside the Pen; those who occupy themselves with the secret of the heart, leaving aside the heart; and those who occupy themselves with the most hidden mystery, leaving aside the secret; and there are those of My servants who wander.[12] Be from whatever class of servants you want."

Then He said to me, "The Leg is a part of the Watchtower (*maṭlaʿ*) and you are above the Watchtower.[13] So why do you concern yourself with the Leg? The Leg depends on you, and moves towards you; and to it clings the man of the Rock."[14]

# *Notes*

1 "The Leg (*sāq*) is the Order (*amr*) which supports that which is built upon it." (IS) See below, n. 13.

According to Sitt al-ʿAjam, the term *sāq* refers to formal manifestation, so that "to reveal a leg" means "to manifest in a form or image (*ṣūra*)".

2 See the verse mentioned above: ". . . and they will be summoned to prostrate." (Q. 68: 42) See Contemplation 6, n. 33.

3 Or support your weight on it.

4 These words "hold onto it and I shall speak to you" allude to a prophetic saying, according to which Moses was clinging to a leg (*sāq*) of the Throne and God spoke to him. (IS) See Contemplation 5, n. 10, and below, n. 13.

5 The Beloved is the Prophet Muhammad.

6 "That is, if something which can be held onto is shown to you, beware of denying what is above it." (IS) Sitt al-ʿAjam, however, considers that this negation may have several meanings, and she explains that this warning may be understood in three ways: (1) beware of denying the image you see, (2) beware of negating the attributes of servanthood, and (3) beware of negating your essence.

7 That is, "we distracted them" using a kind of divine trick (*makr*), by veiling (the servant) from (the vision of) a higher Reality with what is inferior to it. (IS)

8 That is, "the leg follows the foot", and the foot has the meaning of "firmness"; if the foot is firm, the leg is firm, and if not, it stumbles. (IS)

9 "The leg is the Order of God, the Most High, and so by means of it He makes the manifestation of the sun more intense." (IS)

10 "The moon represents the prophets." (IS)

11 The stars refer to what the successive prophets bring of the knowledge of analytical sciences (*ʿulūm al-tafṣīl*), since the prophets are the bearers of distinctive knowledge. Because of this, God the Most High said: ". . . and We sent down to you the reminder (*dhikr*) . . . so that you may explain clearly to people what is revealed to them." (Q. 16: 44) (IS)

12 That is, they do not belong to a particular rank, since they appear in every degree according to what is required by that degree. (IS)

13 "That is, the Leg (*sāq*) is the station of Moses, and the Watchtower (*maṭlaʿ*) is the station of Muhammad. He is on top of the Watchtower, one of whose parts is the leg." (IS)

14 The "man of the Rock" may be an allusion to Moses, who is referred to in the Quranic verse: "He said, 'Did you see when we sought refuge in the rock? Then I forgot the fish . . .'." (Q. 18: 63)

# 8

# Contemplation of the Light of the Rock (*ṣakhra*) as the Star of the Sea (*baḥr*) rises

IN THE NAME OF GOD,
THE COMPASSIONATE, THE MERCIFUL

The Real made me contemplate the Rock[1] and He said to me, "O honourable Rock![2] In you the one who has been nourished by his father's liver seeks refuge,[3] along with he who denies the Green Sea. Tell me, what did he eat when he was on you?"

[The Rock] said, "[He ate] half."[4]

He asked it, "And the other half?"

"It disappeared into the sea", it replied.

He asked, "Dead or alive?"

"Alive", it replied.

He asked, "And the half that was eaten?"

"Dead",[5] it replied.

He asked, "Was it lawful (*ḥalāl*) or unlawful?"

"Lawful", it replied.

"Then say it was alive", He said.

He asked, "How long did they remain sitting[6] on you?"

"All day long", it replied.

He asked, "And during the night?"

It said to Him, "They left me at night[7] and the Green Sea[8] extended over me, covering me with lunar matter;[9] but when it caught sight of the sun, it was pulled away from me and I was uncovered to the sun."

He asked it, "What were the stars doing while the Green Sea was talking to the moon?"

"They fell down and scattered",[10] it replied.

He said to it, "It is right that they did. O moon! Rise from the Sea of the West and when you pass the Dome of Arīn sink down on it; but do not set in the East[11] for you will be driven away."

"O moon! Honour the East by your rising, be it only once in the year!"[12]

"O moon! I forbid you to rise[13] whilst risings and settings remain!"

"O moon! Sink into the Green Sea and only show yourself to its fishes[14] and do not ever emerge!"

"O moon! Tell the Green Sea, by My order, to receive you into its bosom, and not to swell,[15] nor to heave so that its roar may be heard.[16] I am jealously protective of you. Inform it, on My behalf, that if it surges or shows itself or casts you on its shore or hides you from its fishes, I shall give a beast[17] mastery over it so that it drinks it up and then throws it by the rear into nothingness. Then I will take you out of it and plunge you into the White Sea[18] to give it greater offence."

Then He said, "O moon! Tell the rock to let twelve springs[19] pour forth and when they gush out, completely immerse yourself twice[20] in each. Then immerse one third of you[21] in the third, for three is the place of quantity."

"O moon! Do not look at the rock for you will forget what I told you to convey to the Green Sea."

"O moon! Do not sink down on the Dome of Arīn[22] until you become a half-moon; if you were a full moon or a new moon you would not rise, but rise a half-moon without leaving Arīn, and you will know the secret of the rivers, if the High God wills."

# *Notes*

1 See the references in Q. 18: 63 and 31: 16. The rock symbolizes the body and the knowledges it contains, which God has entrusted to it. (IS)
2 This style of address is an allusion to its superiority over the rest of the elements. (SA)
3 The liver is the organ in which blood is produced. In this sense, the heir (*wārith*) is one who has drunk the "blood" of his father. When he says "in you the one who has been nourished by his father's liver seeks refuge" he is also alluding to the heir's affiliation with this earthly aspect. (SA)
4 He ate the half which corresponds to the apparent, whilst the other half returned to its place of origin. (IS)
5 "That is, corresponding to exoteric knowledge." (SA)
6 Those who remained seated are the heirs from the pact of Adam until the present time. (SA)
7 "The day is the place of intimacy between the body and the spirit, so the rock says that they remained seated during the day. The night is the place of withdrawal of the spirit from the body during sleep, so the rock says, 'They left me [at night].'" (IS)
8 "The Green Sea symbolizes knowledge of the essential Reality (*'ilm al-ḥaqīqa*)." (IS)
9 "The moon represents divine knowledge relating to the knowledge of nature. It only covered him with what corresponded to him [by virtue of his nature]." (IS)
10 "That is, when the condition of servanthood is manifested, the adoption [by the servant] of the Names belonging to the condition of lordship, vanishes. The sciences of right guidance belong to the travellers who follow the way and the sciences of the Names belong to those who adopt their characteristics (*mutakhalliqūn*), but when union (*wuṣūl*) is truly reached, these sciences disappear, so that "their stars fall and scatter." (IS)
11 The West is an allusion to knowledge of the mysteries or esoteric knowledge, whilst the East is an allusion to exoteric knowledge. Esoteric knowledge (literally, "the knowledge of the interior") includes the exoteric and has dominion over it, whilst the same is not true of exoteric knowledge. "Do not set in the East" means

"do not invert realities, because the East is not the place of setting; therefore return to the West and set there". (IS)

12 "It is as though He said to the moon: 'Rise one day with the light of your essence, not with accidental light.'" (IS)

13 "That is, O you who are not restricted, I forbid you to manifest with your reality whilst the body continues to rule you." (IS)

14 "That is, to whoever knows you and has a life analogous to yours." (IS)

15 "That is, if such knowledge results in you, do not show it or use it except in its [corresponding] world." (IS)

16 When the sea swells its sound makes its presence evident. Similarly, you must not "get agitated", so that your position remains unknown. This is the greatest state of the Malāmis (*malāmatiyya*: the people of blame) who do not "make waves" and who are not known. (IS)

17 "Beast": one of the parts of the exoteric law which denies the one who talks about esoteric truths. (IS)

18 "The White Sea is the sea of hunger and striving." (IS)

19 An allusion to the signs of the zodiac.

20 The first immersion corresponds to the exterior and the second to the interior; or one immersion for the self (*nafs*) and one for the spirit (*rūḥ*), respectively.

21 That is, your body, in order to realize the complete integration of the three worlds: the self, the spirit and the body. (IS)

22 Arīn is the point of equilibrium, and the moon, in this place of appearance, is an isthmus (*barzakh*) (or a mid-point) between the full moon (*badr*), which is all white, and the new crescent moon (*hilāl*), in which darkness preponderates. (IS) See also Contemplation 3, n. 58.

# 9

# Contemplation of the Light of the Rivers (*al-anhār*) as the Star of Degrees (*rutab*) rises

IN THE NAME OF GOD,
THE COMPASSIONATE, THE MERCIFUL

The Real made me contemplate [the light of] the rivers and He said to me, "Consider their location." I then saw that the rivers led into four seas:[1] the first river flowed into the Sea of Spirits; the second river flowed into the Sea of Speech; the third river flowed into the Sea of the Flute and Intoxication; and the fourth river flowed into the Sea of Love. Little streams branched out from these rivers and irrigated the crops of the sowers.[2]

Then I cast my sight upon the seas and I saw that they ultimately led to one ocean uniting all the seas that flowed into it. I also saw the four rivers gush out from that ocean, then return to it[3] after mixing with these four seas.[4]

Then He said to me, "This ocean is My ocean and those seas are My seas, but the shores claim[5] that they belong to them. The one who sees the ocean before the seas and rivers is veracious.[6] Whoever contemplates them all at once is a witness.[7] Whoever contemplates the rivers, then the ocean and then the seas is a follower of proof,[8] and whoever contemplates the seas, then the rivers, then the ocean has defects but he will be saved."[9]

"I have built a boat[10] for whoever is under My care, so he can make his way in it on the rivers until he reaches their end. When they flow into the seas, he sails on them until at last he reaches the ocean, and when he arrives there he will know the realities, and the secrets will be revealed. To this ocean come those who have been brought close. Those who are above them[11] will sail on it for a thousand years,[12] until they land on its shore. They will disembark in an empty desert[13] without end or limit, and they will wander about in it as long as eternity lasts, and if it ceased they would be extinguished."

Then He said to me, "Look!" And I saw three abodes.[14] He opened the first abode[15] for me and inside I saw some open treasure houses. I also saw the arrows which had struck them repeatedly, and I saw the rabble who roamed around in their vicinity wanting to break them open.[16]

Then I left that abode and He made me enter the second abode,[17] where I saw some locked treasure houses[18] with the keys hanging from their locks. He said to me, "Take the key, open [them], wander through and view!"[19] So I unlocked them and I saw that they were filled with pearls, jewels and garments, which the people of the world would kill each other over, if they were shown them.

Then He said to me, "Take what you need from them and leave them as you found them."

I said, "I have no need of them." So I locked them up.

Then He said "Raise your head," and I saw over their doors, openings and windows which could not be reached except by very tall people, whose height was a hundred cubits or more.[20] I saw those below this height hanging from the knockers of those doors, knocking with them. When the knocking continued and the clamour increased, a fist[21] holding a lamp[22] came out of those windows, illumining them so that they could see one another and become familiar. The wild beasts[23] which had been harming them fled, the snakes withdrew to their holes, and they became safe from all the harm which they had been wary of in the darkness.[24] I also saw arrows stuck into the sides of those treasure houses, although fewer than in the former ones.

Then He brought me to the third abode[25] and made me enter it. I saw locked treasure houses[26] without any keys.

I asked Him, "Where are the keys to these treasure houses?"

"I threw them into the ocean",[27] He replied.

Then He built for me a boat[28] and I sailed on the ocean for six thousand years.[29]

When I was in the seventh millennium, He said to me, "Divest yourself of your clothes[30] for you are in the middle [of the ocean], and plunge after these keys, for here is their 'resting place and [their] place of safekeeping. All is in an evident Book.'"[31]

I took off my clothing and I prepared to remove my loincloth,[32] but He said to me, "If it were not for your loincloth, you would not be able to dive."[33]

So I made fast my loincloth and threw myself from the boat, [diving] until I reached the bottom of the ocean and I gathered up the keys.[34] When I came to the surface of the ocean, fire came out of the keys and it burnt the boat.[35] I travelled back until I arrived at the treasure houses. The keys flew from my hand, rushing to open the locks. I opened the doors and entered the treasure houses where I saw a beginning without any end.[36] I expected to see something inside but I did not see anything except emptiness.

He asked me, "What did you see?"

"I did not see anything", I replied.

He said, "Now you have seen. Every possessor of the secret has spoken from here and this is their bower. Leave!"

I went out and I saw that everything was written on the outside of the doors.[37] Then I noticed that only a few arrows had pierced the sides of the treasure house.

Then He said to me, “Everything you have seen is created and everything created is incomplete. Ascend until you do not see creation.”[38]

I ascended. I threw myself into the sea of perplexity and He left me swimming[39] in it.

# Notes

1 According to Ibn Sawdakīn, Ibn ʿArabī means by the symbol of the seas, the knowledge (*ʿilm*) which the prophets have; and by the four rivers, he means the knowledge of the inheriting saints, who have inherited their respective sciences from the knowledge of Muhammad, Moses, Jesus and David. The Sea of Spirits corresponds to Jesus, the Sea of Speech (or Oration) to Moses, the Sea of the Flute (*mizmār*) and Intoxication to David, and the Sea of Love to Muhammad. See also the reference to the four rivers of water, milk, wine and honey in the Quran (47: 15) and the references in the *Futūḥāt* translated into English by J. W. Morris in *Les Illuminations de La Mecque/The Meccan Illuminations*, pp. 162 and 379 with the corresponding notes (on pp. 536 and 604).

2 These streams or brooks represent what flows from the traditional practice of the learned ones to the travellers on the Way (*sālikūn*). (IS)

3 He means by the ocean the all-encompassing knowledge of God. The gushing of the four rivers from the ocean and their returning to it means that the existence of knowledge in the soul (*nafs*) of an heir is from the side of the Real and only its transmission is due to the Prophet. (IS)

4 An allusion to the fact that the sciences of the heirs do not arise by means of thought (*fikr*), rather they derive from the prophetic inheritance. The prophetic sciences are unadulterated by the sciences which belong to the field of philosophy. (IS)

5 "He means by pretension [or claim] the restriction on which the law (*sharīʿa*) depends and it [the law] binds the jurist." (IS)

6 An allusion to a saying of Abū Bakr: "I have not seen anything without first seeing God." (IS)

7 The spiritual station of ʿUmar Ibn al-Khaṭṭāb (one of the companions of the Prophet who became the second caliph). (IS)

8 That is, he possesses rational evidence.

9 He is saved through having followed the messengers. (IS)

10 That is, the boat of symbolic transposition (*markab al-iʿtibār*). (IS)

11 "He is referring to a group which is higher in rank than those who have been brought close (*al-muqarrabūn*)." (IS)

12 He is alluding to the end of the cycle of ages and the succession of numbers. (IS)

13 "This desert symbolizes perplexity (*ḥayra*)." (IS)

14 These three abodes refer to actions (*afʿāl*), attributes (*ṣifāt*) and essence (*dhāt*). The term "essence" here means the negative attributes (*ṣifāt al-salb*). (IS)

15 That is, the abode of actions. (IS)

16 That is, ignorant people attribute actions to themselves, therefore they associate another agent with God. However, for the great ones, the only means of realizing the contemplation of actions (*mashhad al-fiʿl*) is through the way of witnessing, where the two orders of affirmation and denial are witnessed together, leaving them perplexed. (IS)

The most well-known Quranic reference to this doctrine, which simultaneously affirms and denies the attribution of action to the human being, appears in Q. 8: 17: "You did not throw when you threw, but God threw."

17 The abode of attributes. (IS)

18 The treasures of the attributes. (IS)

19 The word for "view", (*iʿtabir*) can also mean "evaluate" or "take heed and pass beyond to the meaning". See note 10 above and Contemplation 14, n. 22.

20 "The hundred cubits correspond to the hundred Divine Names and their respective theophanies. By saying 'or more' he is referring to a saying of Muhammad: '. . . or You have taken him to Yourself in the knowledge of what is hidden with You [to show him Your favour]' (Ibn Ḥanbal, *Musnad*, I, 391 and 456), which does not mean that the great ones add anything to the hundred." (IS)

21 "The fist represents the eternal power of providential care for that group of people." (IS)

22 "He means by the lamp a special knowledge by which one is rightly guided." (IS)

23 "The wild beasts (*sibāʿ*) [which has the same root as *sabʿa*, 'seven'] represent false images and phantoms." (IS)

24 "That is, unsound speculation." (IS)

25 "The abode of the essence with regard to the negative attributes." (IS)

26 The essential treasures. (IS)

27 Literally, "the encompassing sea (*al-baḥr al-muḥīṭ*)". See above, n. 3.

28 The Real built a boat of remembrance (*dhikr*) and retreat (*khalwa*) for the witness in order that he might see what pertains to the

attribute of transcendence, which is sheer negation. Because of this, fire comes out of the keys which burns the boat of remembrance, retreat and suchlike. (IS)

29 "An allusion to six of the seven divine attributes: life, power, will, speech, sight, hearing – excepting the seventh, knowledge (*ʿilm*), which is the sea itself and embraces everything." (IS)

30 "That is, leave behind your personal attributes." (IS)

31 Q. 11: 6.

32 "The loincloth (*miʾzar*) is what covers the pudenda ... leaving visible what is deposited in trust with humankind." (IS)

33 "That is, if it were not for your trustworthiness (*amāna*) [regarding what God has deposited in you] the essential reality (*ḥaqīqa*) would not be your proper condition." (IS)

34 "That is, I knew the attribute of transcendence." (IS)

35 That is, the attribute of transcendence imposes the command through which everything is annihilated. (IS)

36 "The beginning [of knowledge of the essence] is realizing that it is [something] existent (*mawjūd*) which has no like. Its endlessness is due to the fact that the attribute of transcendence has no end, since you can only declare God's transcendence in relation to accidents and accidents have no end." (IS)

37 "By 'everything' he is alluding to the letter *bāʾ* [the first letter of the Quran and, insofar as it is the beginning, the 'door' (*bāb*) of the revelation]. The letter *bāʾ* or the doors are here the symbol of every attribute that can be attributed to the Real (*al-ḥaqq*)." (IS)

Ibn Sawdakīn's commentary is implicitly alluding to the Sufi tradition according to which the whole of the Quran is contained in the opening Sura (*al-Fātiḥa*), which in turn is contained in the initial letter *bāʾ*, which again is contained in the diacritical point situated below its lower part, that is, "the external face". See Contemplation 11, n. 1.

38 "That is, 'Say, "Lord, increase me in knowledge."' (Q. 20: 114) As for you, where have you been so that creation (*kawn*) does not leave you?" (IS)

39 The root of the Arabic word for "swimming" (*s–b–ḥ*) also means "praising".

# 10

# Contemplation of the Light of Perplexity (*ḥayra*) as the Star of Non-existence (*ʿadam*) rises

IN THE NAME OF GOD,
THE COMPASSIONATE, THE MERCIFUL

The Real made me contemplate [the light of] perplexity and He said to me, "Return!" But I did not find where to. He said to me, "Approach!" But I did not find where. He said to me, "Stop!" But I did not find where.[1] He said, "Do not withdraw!" And I was perplexed.

Then He said to me, "You are you and I am I."[2]
"You are Me and I am you."[3]
"You are not Me and I am not you."[4]
" I am not you and you are Me."
"You are not you, and you are not other than you."
"The I-ness is one and the He-ness (*huwiyya*) is many."[5]
"You are in the He-ness[6] and I am in the I-ness."

Then He said to me, "The witnessing of perplexity is perplexity."
"Perplexity is accompanied by jealousy."[7]
"Perplexity is the reality of reality."[8]
"He who does not remain in perplexity does not know Me."
"He who knows Me does not know what perplexity is."[9]

Then He said to me, "Those who 'stop' get lost in perplexity; and the heirs become realized in it; the followers work towards it; the servants devote themselves to it; the veracious ones speak from it; it is the place from which the envoys are sent and the place of ascent of the aspirations of the prophets."[10]

"Whoever is in perplexity has reached happiness; whoever is in perplexity unifies; whoever unifies exists;[11] whoever exists passes away and whoever passes away remains and whoever remains is worshipped[12] and whoever is worshipped rewards; the One who rewards is the Most High, and the best of the rewards is the I-ness and in it is perplexity."

Then He said to me, "Perplexity is not perplexity. It is only My jealousy towards you. Be jealous of Me and guard Me and veil Me and do not be revealed to other than Me in existence!"

"Make them stay in perplexity and do not point Me out to anyone. Bring them to Me and let them know about Me but do not let them know My place, and let them know about My place[13] without letting them know Me. If they hold fast to My place they will find Me.[14] If they find Me, they will not see anything. If they see something they will not see My place. If they do not see My place, then perhaps they will see Me."

Then He said to me, "This is My garment.[15] Bring it to them. Whoever puts it on[16] is of Me and I am of him. Whoever does not put it on is not of Me and I am not of him."

"Throw it into the fire. If it burns,[17] then it is My garment and if it remains intact then it is not My garment."

"If it burns, it is not My garment, but if it remains intact then it is My garment. Whoever puts on My garment is not of Me, and whoever leaves it is of Me."

"Non-existence bears witness to perplexity: 'I am God; there is no god but I.' "[18]

# Notes

1 "That is, 'I did not find where' to stop because I was absorbed in the contemplation of the Essence which is one entity. If my attention had remained fixed on the Names, I would have been carried away from Name to Name; because if I had returned from that place of contemplation (*mashhad*) I would have fallen into nothingness without realizing it." (IS)

2 "When I told you to return, why did you not return to yourself so that the distinction would prove true, whereby you are you and I am I?" (IS)

3 An allusion to the adoption of the characteristics of the Names (*takhalluq bi-l-asmā'*) by both parties: the Real (*al-ḥaqq*) becomes characterized by the names of the servant like merriment, renunciation and hesitation, and the servant becomes characterized by the names of the Real. (IS)

4 (From the point of view of the transcendent essence) I do not adopt your characteristics nor do you adopt Mine. (IS)

5 The I-ness corresponds to what is expressed by your saying "I", since the first person does not necessitate the existence of any other. However, the He-ness (the hidden reality corresponding to the pronoun "he" or "it" – see Contemplation 6, n. 16) requires the existence of two (the absent one and that from which he is absent), since "hiddenness" (*ghayba*) necessarily occurs in relation to another. (IS)

6 "That is, You are in the hiddenness (the invisible world of what is hidden, *al-ghayb*) because only I manifest from you." (IS)

7 "That is, with the disappearance of otherness, perplexity vanishes." (IS) *Ghayr*, "otherness", comes from the same root as *ghayra*, "jealousy (for another)".

8 "This is the meaning of the saying, '[To realize] the impossibility of attaining knowledge (*idrāk*) is [itself] knowledge." (IS) See also Contemplation 1, n. 23.

9 "That is, he has not been perplexed in other than Me. I have heard my Shaykh Ibn 'Arabī give two explanations about the meaning [of the inability to attain knowledge]. He said, 'When the Veracious One [Abū Bakr] realized his inability [to understand] he needed to rest, because he was the first to perceive this with his own strength,

so he was exhausted; but when he relaxed, his place [of reception – his heart] was empty and the knowledges began to descend on this place which was free and ready to receive.'" (IS)

10 "That is, in the knowledge of God everyone has remained perplexed." (IS)

11 Or "has found".

12 The active and passive voices are ambiguous here: Ibn 'Arabī is alluding to the mystical union of the worshipper and the worshipped.

13 "My place, that is, your existence." (IS)

14 That is, they will find the experiential relationship (literally, "the relationship of taste": *al-nisba al-dhawqiyya*) which exists between your heart and Me. (IS)

15 "The garment or clothing of the Real (*al-ḥaqq*): His attributes and His Names." (IS)

16 Putting on His garment means adorning oneself with the character traits (*takhalluq*) of the Divine Names.

17 Burning means "to stain it with pretension". (IS)

18 This is from the fourteenth verse of the Sura of Ṭā'–Hā' (Q. 20), and was said to Moses when he approached the burning bush. See Contemplation 12, n. 15.

# 11

# Contemplation of the Light of Divinity (*ulūhiyya*) as the Star of *Lām–Alif* rises

IN THE NAME OF GOD,
THE COMPASSIONATE, THE MERCIFUL

The Real made me contemplate [the light] in Divinity as the star of *lām–alif* rose.[1] Explanation is not adequate for it and symbolic language falls short. Description, qualification, name and depiction cease along with "He said", "I said", and "you", and "approach", "go away", "stand up", "sit down", and everything else.

Each thing became clear to me, yet I saw nothing. I saw things, yet I did not see.

The address stopped
    the causes removed
        the veil vanished
Nothing remained but remaining
    annihilation annihilated from annihilation
        by "I"

# *Note*

1 The contemplation of Divinity (*ulūhiyya*) has two aspects like the letter *lām–alif*. The *lām–alif* is written as a single letter (in one continuous line: لا), but it is pronounced as two separate letters (*l* + *ā*). (IS)

Ibn Sawdakīn is alluding to the two aspects of the Divinity which is essentially one and denies the existence of any relationship; yet when it is considered in its creative aspect, Divinity manifests the relationship between the worshipper and the One worshipped.

When the letters *lām* and *alif* are joined in this order (*l* + *ā*) they form the negative particle *lā*, "no", which starts the Quranic formula "*lā ilāha illā anā* [there is] no divinity but I", from the Sura Ṭā'–Hā' (Q. 20: 14). See final line of Contemplation 10.

On the meaning of the letters in general, see D. Gril, "La Science des lettres", in *Les Illuminations de La Mecque*, pp. 383–487, and on the meaning of *lām–alif* and *alif–lām*, in particular pp. 475–80.

# 12

# Contemplation of the Light of Uniqueness (*aḥadiyya*) as the Star of Servanthood (*ʿubūdiyya*) rises

IN THE NAME OF GOD,
THE COMPASSIONATE, THE MERCIFUL

The Real made me contemplate the light of uniqueness as the star of servanthood rose, and He said to me, "Uniqueness is connected to servanthood[1] with the connection of *lām–alif*."

"I am the root[2] and you are the branch."[3]

"The root is you and the branch is 'I'."[4]

Then He said to me, "You are the one and I am the Unique.[5] So whoever goes away from the Uniqueness sees you and whoever stays with it sees himself. This is the presence of continuous succession,[6] which would not be so, if it were divided."[7]

"Only sleep after the odd prayer of the night."[8]

"There are not two odd [prayers] in a night,[9] since [only] one of us subsists."

"Perform the sunset prayer and do not perform the night prayer [on its own] since it is necessary for you to do the odd prayer so that [the number of prostrations] are even."[10]

"I have veiled you with Uniqueness, but if it were not for Uniqueness you would not have known Me and you would not ever know Me."

"Do not profess the unity [of God], else you would be a Christian; if you believe, you are an imitator; if you submit [to Islam] you are a hypocrite; and if you attribute partners to God, you are a Zoroastrian."[11]

Then He said to me, "The delights are in the nourishment, the nourishment in the fruit, the fruit in the boughs which branch out from the trunk and the trunk is one. If it were not for the earth, the trunk would not stand firm; if it were not for the trunk, there would be no branches; if it were not for the branches there would be no fruit; if it were not for the fruit, food would not exist and without food, delight would not exist. So it all depends on the earth; and the earth needs water; water needs the clouds; the clouds need wind, wind is subject to the order,[12] and the order issues from the Lordly Presence. Ascend from here, look, enjoy yourself, but do not speak."[13]

Then He said to me, "Preserve the intermediaries."[14]

"I have written *Ṭā'–Hā'*[15] on the stars of Ursa Minor."[16]

"The Pole of the Right [or south] is the Pole of the Left [or north],[17] and I have set this down in the beginning of the Sura of Iron."[18]

"If there were two Axes (*quṭbān*) the celestial sphere would not turn; and if there were not two Poles (*quṭbān*), the structure would collapse and the celestial sphere would not pursue its course."[19]

Then He said to me, "Do not look at the existence of the Poles, but look at what is hidden in the negation[20] and then say whatever you like, that they are two, or that they are one."

"In the link between *lām* and *alif* there is an undisclosed secret which I have deposited in My saying: 'God is He who raised the heavens without any support.'"[21]

# *Notes*

1 "Servanthood (*ʿubūdiyya*) [which corresponds to the letter *lām*] is necessarily linked to Uniqueness (*aḥadiyya*) [corresponding to the *alif*] because when the High God stood alone in the Uniqueness, this attribute could not be attributed to any other than Him." (IS)

2 Or trunk.

3 In relation to existence, God is the root or origin and the servant is the branch or derivation. (IS)

4 In relation to knowledge (*maʿrifa*) the servant is the root and God is the branch, because you cannot know that you know Him until you know yourself. Therefore knowledge through the servant is the root and knowledge through God branches from it. (IS) See also *Ismail Hakki Bursevi's translation of and commentary on the Fusus al-Hikam by Muhyiddin Ibn 'Arabi*, rendered into English by Bulent Rauf, Vol. 2, p. 484.

5 The unity of the One (*wāḥid*) is a composite oneness, capable of division, whilst the unity of the Unique (*aḥad*) is a simple and indivisible unity.

6 "The presence of continuous succession, since the One manifests in the degrees of the numbers and this manifestation of the unity in the successive numbers [e.g. 1 + 1 + 1 = 3] is the vision of the face of the Real in everything." (IS) Oddness is attributed to God, whilst in creation every odd number is succeeded by an even one, and all created things are in pairs. (See Q. 36: 36, Q. 31: 10, Q. 89: 3.)

7 That is, if it were divided it would no longer be unity, but rather duality (*shafʿiyya*). (IS)

8 This is found in a hadith. (See Wensinck, *Concordance*. Ibn Ḥanbal, 1, 20.) This supererogatory prayer of the night is usually performed alone and consists of an uneven number of ritual movements (*rakaʿāt*), which is why it is called "odd" (*witr*).

"That is, since the sunset prayer (*maghrib*) is also odd, [do the odd prayer] to complete an even number of ritual movements (*rakaʿāt*) so that by making oddness even, you go to sleep with your attribute [i.e. evenness, *shafʿiyya*] and not with Mine." (IS) According to a well-known hadith, "God is *witr* and loves the *witr*."

It is also reported in a hadith (Bukhārī, 21, 248) that the Prophet's wife, ʿĀ'isha, asked the Prophet whether he slept before the *witr* prayer and he replied, "O 'Ā'isha, my eyes sleep, but my heart remains awake." According to another hadith (Bukhārī, 21, 274), Abū Hurayra was advised by the Prophet to do three things, one of which was "to offer *witr* before sleeping." Yet a third hadith (Abū Da'ūd, 8, 1429) narrates how the Prophet asked Abū Bakr when he observed the *witr* prayer. Abū Bakr replied, "I observe the *witr* prayer in the early hours of the night." The Prophet then asked 'Umar when he observed the *witr* and he replied, "At the end of the night." The Prophet then said, regarding Abū Bakr, "This one has followed it with care"; and regarding 'Umar, "He has followed it with strength."

9 This is also from a hadith. (Bukhārī, *Witr* 4.)

10 According to another hadith, "the sunset prayer is the odd prayer of the day". The obligatory night prayer has an even number of ritual movements, so the supererogatory odd prayer (*witr*) of the night is therefore necessary to balance the odd prayer of the day. ("The *witr* is necessary." See Ibn Ḥanbal, 5, 315.)

The matter of oddness and the night prayer has many aspects and this passage is ambiguous. Ibn 'Arabī devotes a long section to the *witr* prayer in the *Futūḥāt*. See Osman Yahia edition, Vol. 7, pp. 250–71. See also Contemplation 4, n. 25.

11 Here, Ibn 'Arabī is using provocative expressions of a kind often used by Sufis to explain the degree of annihilation in the Unity (*al-fanā' fī'l-tawḥīd*). For example, there is a famous passage, collected by Abū Naṣr al-Sarrāj (d. 988–89) in his work *Luma'*, p. 50, in which, on being asked about pure Unity as an expression of a unique reality, Shiblī (d. 846) replied: "Alas! Whoever replies about *tawḥīd* using clear statements is a deviator, whoever alludes to it is a dualist, whoever is silent about it is ignorant, whoever presumes that he has arrived has not attained, whoever points it out is an idol worshipper, whoever speaks of it is unaware, whoever thinks he is near is distant, and whoever thinks he has found, loses. Everything that you distinguish through your imagination or perceive through your intellect, however complete, comes from you and returns to you: it is contingent and fabricated like you." See S. Hakim, *al-Mu'jam al-ṣūfī*, "*al-ilāh al-makhlūq*" (the divinity created [in the beliefs]).

12 An allusion to the verse: "We subjected the wind to him, to blow gently to his order . . .". (Q. 38: 36)

13 This paragraph explains that existents are disposed according to two ways: from the root (or origin) to the branch (or derivation), and vice versa. The way of the people of insight (*kashf*) begins with the Real (*al-ḥaqq*), through whose Light existence is then revealed. However, the way of the people who rely on rational proofs starts from the creation perceived through the senses and the faculty of speculative thought, then ascends to the Real by means of symbolic transposition (*iʿtibār*) and reflection (*fikr*). (IS)

14 That is, I have established the intermediaries, so understand why I have established them. (IS)

15 These two separate characters form the first verse of the twentieth sura of the Quran, hence its title. The sum of the numerical value of both letters is fourteen (9 + 5 = 14), that is, the number of chapters which make up this book. These letters, like other groups of enigmatic letters found in the Quran, are read separately by their names. Ṭā'–Hā' is also one of the names of the Prophet and as such refers to the "Reality of Muhammad". See Contemplations 10, n. 18 and 11, n. 1.

16 Ursa Major symbolizes the universe whilst Ursa Minor, in which the Pole (Star) (*quṭb*) appears, symbolizes the copy of the universe. (IS) Each of these constellations is characterized by seven particularly bright stars. The Pole Star is the ancient means of orientation used to determine the direction in which to pray at night. It lies between Capricorn and the stars Beta and Gamma in Ursa Minor. It was considered to be the star upon which the sphere turns, because it never changes position. It was also compared to the axle of a millstone.

17 In the character *lām–alif*, which consists of two vertical lines joined at the bottom, the line corresponding to the *alif* is on the left and that which corresponds to the *lām* is on the right. However, since they are joined, they may be considered as a single line.

18 An allusion to the verse which says: "He is the First and the Last, the Exterior and the Interior." (Q. 57: 3)

19 For this reason, there are two "Axes" or "Poles" (*quṭbān*) united in one character, *lām–alif*.

20 The character *lām–alif*, meaning "no".

21 "God is He who raised the heavens without any support that you can see . . ." (Q. 13:2)

# 13

# Contemplation of the Light of the Support (*'amd*) as the Star of Singularity (*fardāniyya*) rises

IN THE NAME OF GOD,
THE COMPASSIONATE, THE MERCIFUL

The Real made me contemplate the light of the Support as the star of singularity[1] rose, and He said to me, "I have hidden him[2] from sight in annihilation and I have revealed him in subsistence. I have hidden him in what is manifest and revealed him in what is hidden and concealed."

Then He said to me, "I have revealed you in annihilation, and covered the looks with veils so that they do not perceive him."

"I have set up the dome,[3] fixed the support in the centre, and made firm the stakes.[4] I have allowed everyone in existence entrance."

Some were veiled by the dome itself, by its exquisiteness and beauty. Others were veiled by the stakes and they clung to them. Some were veiled by the ropes[5] of the dome and stayed with them. Others were veiled by the furnishings and contents. But none of them saw the support of the dome until a group entered who said, "A dome with no support is inconceivable." So they searched until they found the support. Then they looked to see in what way the others were veiled from the support, and they found covers over their eyes. So they seized the support, and when they got a grip on it they tore it out of the ground and took it away, so that the dome fell on those who remained.

Then He said to me, “If only you had seen them rolling around in it, colliding and hurting each other, not being guided, just like fish in the fisherman’s net! When I saw them thrashing about, I sent fire down on them and burnt them, and I burnt the dome with its fixings, furnishings and stakes. Then I revived them and said to them, ‘Look at what you were holding onto.’ They looked and found scattered dust.”[6]

Then He said to me, “Be with the companions of the Support.[7] If you are not with them you will perish and if you are their companion, you will perish.”[8]

“Whoever sees the Support[9] has been veiled.[10] Beware of argument, for it brings perdition!”

# *Notes*

1 Nothing is brought into being directly from the One (*aḥad*); rather, existence comes about from oddness or singularity (*fardiyya*), because existence only comes about from the relationship of three; see Contemplation 1, n. 14. For this reason, it is given expression through the word "*kun*" (Be!) which has three letters (*k–w–n*) (IS) See Contemplation 2, n. 13.

The three letters of the creative word correspond to (1) the One in relation to Its Essence, (2) the relationship of the One to the World, and (3) the link which connects both aspects of the One. This third aspect is related to the Support who is hidden from sight, like the letter *wāw* in the word "*kun*" (from the root *k–w–n*) since it does not appear in writing in the Arabic. In addition, the letter *wāw* signifies "and", which is the link between two aspects.

For further explanation on this subject, see *K. al-Mīm wa-l-wāw wa-l-nūn*, pp. 10–12.

2 "Him" refers to the Support (*ʿamd*) or Pole who is the Perfect Man (*al-insān al-kāmil*). (IS)

The term *ʿamd* means "support", "prop" and hence, "column" or "pillar" (*ʿamūd*) – and it also means "intention" or "purpose". According to Ibn ʿArabī, the Perfect Man, the Support, is the purpose of creation.

3 The dome (*qubba*) symbolizes the worldly existence, or everything which one clings to besides God. (IS)

4 The term used for "stakes" (*awtād* – tent peg, pole) is also used to refer to the four "Pillars" of the spiritual hierachy, namely, the Pole, the Imām of the Left, the Imām of the Right and the Fourth Pillar.

5 The term "*asbāb*", (tent) ropes, also means secondary causes.

6 A Quranic expression which appears in the verse: "We shall come to the deeds they have done and We shall make them as scattered dust." (Q. 25: 23)

7 MS. B says, "Be with those who preceded [you] in the company ("withness", *maʿiyya*) and in oneness (*ittiḥād*)."

8 "That is, be with the One whom they are with, not with them [literally, "be with their 'withness' (company) not with their selves"] for if you are in their company you are with the One whom they are with, not with them." (IS) See Contemplation 14, n. 14.

9 That is, whoever sees the Support and stays with him. (IS)

10 The human being has been created with a natural disposition for travelling. So if he stops at a time which is not right, he retrogrades. It is more suitable for him to move forward in his journey, not fall behind, so that he is in increase, not in lack. (IS)

# 14

# Contemplation of the Light of Argument (*ḥijāj*) as the Star of Justice (*ʿadl*) rises

IN THE NAME OF GOD,
THE COMPASSIONATE, THE MERCIFUL

The Real made me contemplate the light of argument[1] as the star of justice rose. I saw that the earth had been flattened and had cast out what was in it and become empty.[2]

He said to me, "O My servant, observe what I do with people [inclined to] quarrel and dispute, vain desires and innovation. I am the All-Vanquisher."

I saw a pavilion pitched there, whose [central] support (*ʿamūd*) was of fire and whose sides and ropes were of tar.

He said to me, "This pavilion is for you. Am I to be an object of dispute?[3] Or can I be spoken of by anyone but Myself?[4] Are they capable of defining Me? How absurd are their imaginings! Let them have what they deserve!"[5]

Then He said to me, "O My servant, when the adherents of different factions enter this pavilion, decide which is yours, go with them, and if they are saved, you are saved and if they perish, you perish. Lend hearing and witness! This is the Balance of Justice which has been set up and the Path of Truth which has been extended, the Hell of Discord which has been kindled and the Paradise of Agreement which has been brought near."[6]

Then came the call, "Where are the rationalists with their pretensions?"

The philosophers were brought forward with their followers and were made to enter the pavilion. They were asked, "To what have you applied your intellect?" They replied, "To what pleases You."

He said, "How do you know [what pleases Me]? Just by the intellect or by following and conformity [to the prophets]?"

"Through our intellects alone", they replied.

He said, "You did not understand and you did not succeed; you passed your own judgement. O Fire, pass judgement on them!"

I heard their cries of woe from the layers of fire. "Who is punishing them?", I asked.

He said to me, "Their intellect, since that is what they worshipped. No one questioned them except themselves, and no one punished them other than themselves."

Then came the call, "Where are the naturalists?"

They were brought forward and I saw four rough and strong angels[7] with curved sticks in their hands.

They asked, "O Angels of God, what do you want from us?"

[The angels] said, "To destroy you and torment you."

"But why?", they asked.

[The angels] replied, "When you were in the world, you claimed that we were your gods and you worshipped us to the exclusion of God and you considered actions came from us. God has given us power over you [so that] we may torment you in the fire of Hell." Then they were thrown headlong into it.

Then came the call, "Where are the materialists (*al-dahriyya*)?"[8]

They were brought and they were told, "You are those who profess: 'And only Time (*dahr*) can destroy us.'[9] Didn't your innermost feelings tell you that you would arrive in this place?"

They replied, "No, our Lord."

He said, "Didn't the envoys bring you indisputable evidence? You denied it and said, 'God did not reveal anything.'[10] Away with you, for you have no excuse!" They were thrown headlong into the fire of Hell.

Then came the call, "Where are the Muʿtazilites,[11] who strayed from the straight path?"

They were all brought forward together, and they were told, "You laid claim to lordship saying, 'we do as we like'."[12] Then they were cast headlong into the fire of Hell.

Then came the call, "Where are the spiritualists?"

They were brought forward and I saw that of all the people they were the most hideous and the most maliciously joyful at others' misfortune, except for one group [who had] separated from them under the protection of the prophets and veracious ones, beneath the pavilion of safety.

He said to me, "Join with them if you want salvation and follow their path. But do not join with them (*maʿa-hum*) whilst the [final] *mīm* remains.[13] When the *mīm* disappears, join with them whilst the 'withness'[14] remains, and when the 'withness' disappears, do as you like and it will not be held against you."

I saw that seven groups of spiritualists had been questioned and become veiled, for their passions had played with them and Satan had seduced them. All the [other] groups took refuge [in God] from them and from their punishment, and [the seven groups] fell between layers of fire.

Then they were told, "This is what you disbelieved in. Where is your divine nature now to intercede on behalf of your human nature? 'Say, Truth has come and falsehood has passed away.'"[15]

I entered the Garden with the eighth group. I eliminated the "*mīm*" as He had told me, and the "withness" remained with seventy thousand veils. The "withness" did not cease traversing the veils and rending them until it disappeared in the last veil, so that no veil nor "withness" remained.

Then the eighth group exclaimed, "Our Lord, give us what You have promised us!"[16]

The servant[17] who is needy of the mercy of his Lord said:

So He revealed Himself to [each of] them in the form of [their own] knowledge; and the visions differed, some being more excellent than others.[18]

He said to me, "This is your form,[19] show yourself to them in it."

Then He said to me, "Enter the pavilion and its fire will revert to light. Enter the flames and it will turn into Paradise. Do not enter a place except through Me and do not seek anything but Me."

The arguments rose up against the people of argument, and [the question] was asked, "Who is saved?"

I said, "Whoever did not have an argument."

He said, "'Say: To God is the decisive argument, and if He had wanted, He would have guided you all.'[20] So the one who follows [God's] argument is saved."

Then He said to me, "Return and inform [the others]: 'Magnify [Me]! And cleanse your garments and abandon what is impure!'[21] And in this station, be warned and pass beyond!"[22]

Then He said to me, "Do not do anything that I have told you to do. If you do not do it, you will perish and if you do it, you will perish. So be on your guard and do not depart from the Order!"

# *Notes*

1 MS. J reads: "The Real made me contemplate the Presence of Argument." The argument is related to the Day of Judgement.
2 He is referring to the valley of reunion on the Day of Judgement (*al-sāhira*), implying that people are awake (*sāhir*). See Q. 84: 3–4.
3 This is a reprimand to those who make God an object of debate. According to a well-known saying of the Prophet, God has expressly forbidden theorizing about His Essence, since the Divine Essence is not a matter for speculation.
4 That is, "Can I be known through the words of other than Me?" God warns people not to attribute to Him anything except what He has attributed to Himself through revelation.
5 Literally, "May their hands perish through what they have earned!"
6 See Q. 81: 12–13.
7 The four angels seem to refer to the four elements of Nature.
8 *Al-dahriyya*: *dahr* literally means time. In Islam an adherent of the *dahriyya* is a materialist or atheist.
9 Q. 45: 24.
10 Q. 67: 9.
11 The Muʿtazilites ("those who keep themselves apart") believed that truth could be reached through rational argument and disputation.
12 This is an allusion to what the Muʿtazilites say about the independence of the human will and the human being's autonomous control over the power to do what he wants.
13 The letter *mīm* is transliterated as "m". When the final "m" or *mīm* of *maʿa-hum* ("with them") is taken away, the expression *maʿa-hu* ("with Him") remains. The "withness" (*maʿiyya*) requires company and were it not for company, there would be no argument. (IS)
14 The "withness" (*maʿiyya*) refers to the verse from the Sura of Iron: "He is with you wherever you are." (Q. 57: 4)
15 Q. 17: 81.
16 Q. 3: 194.
17 The term *ʿabd* (servant) is used again here in another "unveiling", in this case concerning the meeting on the Day of Judgement. Once more it emphasizes the ontological indigence of the servant in relation to God. See Contemplation 3, n. 21.
18 An allusion to the well-known hadith, according to which God will

show Himself to each person on the Day of Resurrection in the form in which he knows Him, and due to this, each vision differs in superiority.

19 That is, the form of your knowledge of God.

20 Q. 6: 149.

21 Q. 74: 3–5.

22 The word for "be warned and pass beyond" (*iʿtabir*) also means "cross over to the hidden significance". See Contemplation 9, n. 19.

# APPENDICES

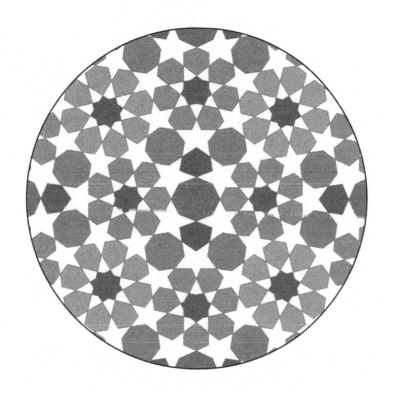

# 1

## The manuscripts used in the edition of the text[1]

Many manuscript copies of the *Contemplation of the Holy Mysteries* have been preserved, both in public and private libraries, along with the contributions of commentators who have annotated the work. In order to arrive at the Arabic text on which this translation is based, Souad Hakim and Pablo Beneito selected three manuscript copies. These are all early copies, written within fifty years of Ibn ʿArabī's death. They were considered to be the most complete and significant copies, enabling the original writing of the author to be reconstructed in the most reliable way.

1. The copy which is used as the basis of this edition appears in a miscellaneous codex of the Manisa library in Turkey, MS. no. 1183, fols. 47b–83b, dated AH 686/1287. The copy is in good condition, although it is not vocalized and contains few diacritical marks. After the text of the *Mashāhid*, there is a brief and succinct explanation of some of the terms and sentences contained in the preface and in the text of the *Contemplations* itself. Judging by the style and by the tone which the author adopts in the conclusion to this commentary, these brief annotations may well be notes dictated by Ibn ʿArabī himself.[2]

1. See Hakim and Beneito, *Contemplaciones*, pp. XX–XXIII.
2. See O. Yahia, *Répertoire Générale* (R.G.) 684.

2. The second copy, called "B" in the notes to this edition, belongs to the Fatih library (Turkey), MS. no. 5322, fols. 201a–214a. This is a commentary written by Ibn Sawdakīn in AH 646/1248 from notes taken from oral explanations by Ibn ʿArabī. This copy also includes a commentary on the *Kitāb al-Isrāʾ*, another work of a visionary and ascendant nature which is intimately related to the text of the *Contemplations*. The complete title of this double commentary is *Kitāb al-Najāt min ḥujub al-ishtibāh fī sharḥ mushkil al-fawāʾid min kitāb al-isrāʾ wa ʾl-mashāhid*. One of the other texts included in this manuscript codex is dated AH 947/1540.

3. The third copy, represented by the letter "J", is MS. no. 2019 of the Ayasofia library, Turkey, fols. 100a–392b, *Kashf al-kunūz fī sharḥ al-mashāhid al-qudsiyya*,[3] which includes a commentary by Sitt al-ʿAjam bint al-Nafīs b. Abū al-Qāsim (died about 1288) on the *Contemplations*. This original manuscript is dated AH 686/1287.

Sitt al-ʿAjam states in her commentary on the *Contemplations*[4] that she voluntarily refrains from explaining its structure.[5]

3. See Yahia, R.G. 337 and 432.

4. S. Hakim and B. Aladdin have recently published a critical edition of this work. See Bibliography.

5. See Chodkiewicz, *Ocean*, p. 56, n. 9.

# 2

## Ibn ʿArabī's preface

The preface is written in the form of a letter addressed to the companions of Shaykh ʿAbd al-ʿAzīz al-Mahdawī and especially to Ibn ʿArabī's paternal cousin, ʿAlī b. al-ʿArabī. The letter points out the merits of some of Mahdawī's teachings. In particular, it elaborates on a statement by him that "the knowledgeable ones of this community are the prophets of other communities" in relation to a saying of the Prophet Muhammad that "the knowledgeable ones are the heirs of the prophets."

Ibn ʿArabī emphasizes the continuity of divine inspiration and refers to the secrets which have been bestowed on the saints. His intention is clearly to deflect possible opposition to controversial statements such as "God made me contemplate . . . and He said to me . . . and I said to Him", by explaining what the divine speech is. Ibn Sawdakīn did not provide any notes on the preface in his commentary since, he writes, it is only "an introduction and a foreword containing some useful teachings regarding the virtues of Shaykh ʿAbd al-Azīz al-Mahdawī; it is perfectly clear and transparent and requires no introduction."[1] However, it includes several ideas which are particularly relevant and clarifying for the reading of the *Contemplations* and the following is a brief account of these, translated from the summary made by Souad Hakim and Pablo Beneito in the Arabic/Spanish edition of the *Contemplations*.[2]

1. See Chodkiewicz, *Quest*, p. 28.

2. See Hakim and Beneito, *Contemplaciones*, pp. VI–XIII. It has been slightly adapted.

Ibn ʿArabī makes it clear from the outset that this book is an inspired work. The author says:

> The [divine] address reached me from the Presence of the [hidden] Identity (*ḥaḍrat al-huwiyya*), making this writing appear and take form in the sensory world. By that I wish to make known that this book has descended from the Presence of Holiness to reveal itself to the precious essence[3] [. . .]
> I was told "Take it with strength and make it known to everyone you see; verify it, examine it thoroughly and be precise [in communicating it], and if anyone asks you, 'How can you claim that it is a revealed work, inspired by the divine speech, if after Muhammad [according to Islamic tradition] there can be no more [prophetic] inspiration (*waḥy*)?', then reply: 'Although Gabriel, the Angel of Revelation, no longer descends after the ending of the prophetic cycle, that does not mean that [divine] inspiration (*ilhām*) has ceased descending on the hearts of the saints (*awliyā'*) [. . .], because divine Reality (*al-ḥaqq*) has not ceased, nor will it cease to inspire them with His mysteries (*asrār*), making the suns and moons of His knowledge rise in the sky of their hearts. The sudden illuminations (*mawārid*) which God causes to arrive in their hearts are infinite and unlimited, like oceans without shores [. . .].'"
>
> He made me stop[4] in the same way that He has made every heir and gnostic stop, and imparted to me the divine secrets in the places of contemplation (*mashāhid*) and the stopping places (*mawāqif*) and established me among those who have access to unveiling and manifestation, and made me come and go between the Lotus Tree of the Extreme Limit and the Visited House and this is the degree of verification conforming to the way of the traces of the prophets.

3. This expression (*al-jawhar al-nafīs*) alludes also to the "substance" or "jewel" (*jawhar*) and to the creative Divine Breath (*nafas*).

4. Stop, pause or stay – as in Niffarī's *Book of Spiritual Stayings* (*Mawāqif*).

The author defends the diversity of inspiration by saying that, just as God sent down the Torah, the Gospels, the Pages (*ṣuḥuf*)[5] and the Quran (*tanzīl*) in successive revelations, when a single book may have sufficed, so He enlightens His saints with various inspirations, revealing to one what He does not reveal to another, so that some illuminations are more complete than others.

Moreover, Ibn 'Arabī points out that the transmission of the inspirations is necessary, since if everyone who receives inspired knowledge were to receive a private and exclusive illumination which could not be conveyed to others, then there would be no communication or mutual understanding. Consequently, in a case where true discernment based on mystical experience (*dhawq*) did not exist, nor the proof conferred by authentic illumination, any ignorant person could set about preaching incoherent doctrines affirming that they are an irrefutable divine revelation.

As Ibn 'Arabī explains, the knowledge of the secrets that is granted to the saints or friends of God depends on the height of the spiritual station which they have reached. Among them are those whom God has endowed with the perception of satanic tricks and the machinations of the (lower) self, and also those who pay attention to the power of the passions, observing the mastery that these exercise over human beings. Each friend of God knows, definitively, what his station bestows on him.

Commenting on the interconnectedness of the spirits and the fact that the spirit is linked with all existence, without being measured in terms of time and space, Ibn 'Arabī observes, "Whoever the world of the spirits has been revealed to, and who sees the connectedness and direct relationship between them, and that there is no separation between them nor time for them, it is easy for him to hear in this way . . ." , that is, as in the speech heard in the *Contemplations*.[6]

5. According to Lane's *Arabic–English Lexicon* these are the Books revealed to Abraham and Moses. See also Q. 87: 19.

6. He also mentions a tradition according to which Sāriya hears the voice of 'Umar b. al-Khaṭṭāb, who warned him of the enemy in advance by calling, "O Sāriya, look to the mountains!" when there was several days' distance between them.

The wise ones who have "arrived" are of two kinds: those who return and those who do not. Those who do not return are called by the name *wāqif* (the one who stops) among the Sufis. Those who return are also divided into two: those whose return is particular, who are called knowers (*ʿārif*), and those whose return is general, who are called heirs.

Since the *Contemplations* contains expressions like "God the Real made me witness a vision and said to me . . . and I said to Him", and similar expressions which could engender doubt, Ibn ʿArabī found himself obliged to comment on his experience in this "station of the word" and to explain what the reception of the divine speech is, in order to stop those who are ignorant of mystical realities from impugning his doctrine.

On speaking of [divine] words in the context of his work, the Shaykh refers to the meanings which appear in the soul, not to voices or letters. He says:

> The Maker (*al-Bāri'*), Glory to Him, is far above the existence of voices and letters in His essence; rather He, Glory to Him, is speaking unconditionally through the ancient speech which is an attribute of meaning that He has attributed to Himself. One does not say that it is Him nor that it is other than Him . . . His speech, Glory to Him, is far above voice or letter, priority or posteriority. Every word which appears in existence is newly arrived, and it is His creation and invention.

It remains clear, then, that "this speech is in reality the speech of the self (*kalām al-nafs*), and the words, writing, symbols and allusions are its indications and are not the speech itself" [. . .] "Why do you think this speech without voice or letter is implausible when you talk to yourself about what has happened without voice or letter all the time? It is speech as it really is and the tongue is its interpreter . . . The Arab poet says, 'Verily speech is in the heart, the tongue only indicates what is in it.'"

The place of reception of the inspirations and arrivals is the heart. Ibn 'Arabī quotes the hadith, "Neither My heavens nor My earth encompass Me but the heart of My servant contains Me." The heart's vastness and boundless ability to receive forms or images of contemplations is then confirmed when he says:

> The heart of the gnostic has no discernible limit and is the seat of God's vision through the servant and the place of His divine revelation, the Presence of His secrets, the place to which His angels descend and the treasury of His lights . . . The forms of the meanings appear to the people of this way in the depths of their hearts . . . so they contemplate the divine impressions and the secrets of predestination and how it holds sway over the created beings.

This book of *Contemplations* is from the sciences of the mysteries (*'ulūm al-asrār*) which are only revealed to the contemplative mystics, since they flow from the source of the secret of "the confirmation of truth (*ṣiddīqiyya*)". This is the class of secrets to which a disciple of Abū Yazīd al-Bisṭāmī alluded when he said, "I have carried three hundred words taken from Abū Yazīd to my grave, because I never found anyone worthy of them." Although these secrets are not disclosed [directly except to those who are able to receive them], it is not forbidden to reveal them and communicate them, as Niffarī, Abū Mūsā al-Dubaylī, Ibn Barrajān of Seville and Ibn al-'Arīf have done in their works.

Finally, Ibn 'Arabī observes that these secrets are protected so that they cannot be discovered in a casual way, without proper attention. On the contrary, he says, earnest endeavour and constant application are required, accompanied by great yearning and a submissive heart.

## *Other works mentioned in the preface*[7]

In the preface to the *Contemplations* (R.G. 432), Ibn ʿArabī on two occasions mentions his own *al-Tadbīrāt al-ilāhiyya* (R.G. 716) and, on another two, the still unedited *Īḍāḥ al-ḥikma* by Abū al-Ḥakam Ibn Barrajān of Seville. He also mentions reading the *Lawāmiʿ anwār al-qulūb fī asrār al-ḥubb wa ʾl-maḥbūb*, by Abū al-Qāsim Shaydhala, and indirectly (referring to the author as *ṣāḥib al-mawāqif*) the *Mawāqif* by Niffarī, probably the work which exercised most influence on the conception and writing of the *Contemplations* (*mashāhid*). In addition, in the *faṣl khātimat al-kitāb*, the Epilogue to the book, Ibn ʿArabī mentions three of his former works, the *Kitāb jalāʾ al-qulūb* (R.G. 166), the *Kitāb al-Jamʿ wa ʾl-tafṣīl fī maʿānī al-tanzīl* (R.G. 172) and the *Kitāb al-Taḥqīq ʿan al-sirr al-ladhī waqara fī nafs al-Ṣiddīq* (R.G. 751), three treatises which have apparently been lost.

7. See Hakim and Beneito, *Contemplaciones*, pp. IV–V.

# 3

## Ibn ʿArabī's epilogue

The epilogue is really an appendix whose function is, as Ibn ʿArabī tells us, to corroborate the mystical revelations and holy contemplations described in the main text. He does this by quoting verses from the Quran, sayings of the Prophet Muhammad and referring to other traditional teachings which provide the foundation for Islamic instruction.[1] The quotations he chooses confirm that knowledge is given by God and is revealed in the heart according to the heart's purity and clarity, where it appears as a shining light.

The following section includes the quotations cited in the Arabic/Spanish version, together with some additional passages.[2] Among the Quranic verses which Ibn ʿArabī mentions are the following:

> . . . and We have shown them a knowledge [coming] from Us.[3]

> Revere God and He will teach you.[4]

> . . . and he who was dead and We revived him giving him a light with which to walk among the people.[5]

1. See Hakim and Beneito, *Contemplaciones*, p. XVI.

2. See also the new French/Arabic edition by S. Ruspoli (Actes Sud, 1999), which includes a French translation of the Epilogue. The Ruspoli edition is based on an undated manuscript of the *Mashāhid* which is followed by a commentary by Qūnawī, Chester Beatty Library Dublin, no. 5493 (text: fols. 25a–50b; commentary: fols. 50b–83a) and has been checked against an eighteenth-century manuscript from the Bibliothèque Nationale, Paris, no. 6104 (fols. 1–75, dated AH 1076). It differs in many places from the critical edition on which our translation is based.

3. Q. 18: 65.

4. Q. 2: 282.

5. Q. 6: 122.

He also comments on the following traditions of the Prophet, among others:

> Whoever acts according to what he knows, God makes him heir to knowledge that he did not know.
>
> Knowledge (*ʿilm*) is a light which God puts in the heart of whoever He pleases.

He quotes a well-known hadith about the proximity reached by means of free acts, in which God speaks through the mouth of the Prophet: ". . . and My servant does not cease to draw near to Me through supererogatory works until I love him. And when I love him, I am the hearing with which he hears and the sight by which he sees."[6]

This is followed by another hadith about the heart, "Hearts are containers. In an open heart is a lamp which shines and that is the heart of the believer."

As for sayings of the companions of the Prophet, Ibn ʿArabī reports that ʿAlī struck his chest with his hand and said, "Here are knowledges in abundance – if only I could find someone to bear them." After mentioning and commenting on several other references, Ibn ʿArabī returns to the heart (*qalb*) as a receptacle for knowledge, describing its many facets and its constant transformation (*taqallub*).[7] He says, "When the High God wishes to

6. The hadith continues, "the hand with which he takes hold and the foot with which he walks. If he asks Me, I give to him; if he seeks refuge in Me, I grant it. In nothing do I hesitate so much as I hesitate [to take] the soul of a believer. He has a horror of death and I have a horror of harming him."

7. He mentions how the heart is like a round mirror with six faces (*awjuh*: faces, facets or aspects), although there is a divergence of opinion among the people of truths and unveilings, since some say the heart has eight faces. Ibn ʿArabī says no attention should be paid to anyone who claims there are nine faces, as Divine Wisdom prevents that. However, it is possible to affirm that "the heart has an indefinite number of aspects just as the Divine Majesty has an innumerable number of attributes." This matter is a subtle one which only people of taste can understand. Ibn ʿArabī adds that he has discussed this question at length in his book entitled *The Polishing of Hearts* (*Jalāʾ al-qulūb*). He hastens to refute any possible objection that

grant his servant some of these [special] knowledges, He takes charge of the mirror of his heart through His grace (*tawfīq*), He looks at it with the eye of benevolence (*luṭf*) and help (*tawfīq*), and supports it with the sea of strong backing (*ta'yīd*)." He then describes how the various facets of the heart are each polished in turn, so that the mirror of the heart becomes clear and free from the rust of otherness. Then the revelation which appears in the heart varies according to the heart's readiness to receive forms.

The Divine Presences towards which the various facets of the heart are turned contain exoteric mysteries and esoteric mysteries. The former belong to the people of progress by degrees and the latter to the people of the realities, for, as Ibn 'Arabī points out, not every "wise person" is truly wise: "The truly wise person is governed by wisdom and bound by his occupation with the decisive speech and his refraining from looking towards anything other than his Creator; for this, vigilance is necessary at every moment. Someone who speaks of wisdom without its effects being evident in him is not called wise."

He then quotes a saying of the Prophet, "Lord, the carrier of a knowledge is not an expert in it – rather, it is left in trust with him so that he is led to something else, 'like the donkey who carries sacred books'."[8] In order to establish whether you are the possessor of a knowledge which arises in you, or merely its carrier, it is necessary to observe how it manifests within yourself: "To verify this, look at your being rightly guided in the clearest way, the soundest road and the most preferable balance in your words, deeds and heart."

Ibn 'Arabī then describes the seven degrees of rectitude, "proper direction" or "being rightly guided" (*istiqāma*) according to the appropriateness of words, actions and the state of the heart. The most excellent degree is appropriateness of words, actions and

what he is saying is contrary to Abū Ḥāmid al-Ghazālī's teaching, "It is not possible to have a more beautifully constructed world than this one."

8. Q.62:5.

heart, followed by appropriateness of actions and heart but not words, and then various combinations of these.

Finally, Ibn ʿArabī points out that the reasons why people are diverted from the way of perfect rectitude are innumerable. He warns his reader to beware of the ruse of God, for "no one feels safe from the ruse of God except those who are lost."[9]

He cites the words of protection given by the Prophet when he prayed to God, "I ask you to forgive what I know and what I do not know" and relates the Prophet's response on being asked if he was afraid – he replied, "What can I trust in, since the heart is between the two fingers of the All-Compassionate and He twiddles it as He wishes?"

Ibn ʿArabī again quotes from the Quran, "But God will show them something they did not expect",[10] and explains that "the human being is the place of change and he receives every attribute that comes upon him . . . so be on your guard while you remain in your bodily composition." This echoes the final words of the *Contemplations*, where the warning is given, "So be on your guard and do not depart from the Order!"

He quotes some words that he attributes to the Torah[11] in which God addresses Moses by saying, "Oh, son of Adam! Do not think you are safe from My ruse until you have traversed the path." He affirms that "The straight path is finer than a hair and sharper than a sword: no one can adhere to it except the people under God's special care."[12] He concludes by saying, "If you wish to reach the lights and secrets [of such people], follow in their footsteps."

9. Q.7:99.
10. Q.39:47.
11. Presumably deriving from some rabbinical commentary.
12. See Contemplation 9: "I have built a boat for those who are [literally] 'of the people in my care.'" Earlier in the Epilogue he states that these knowledges of Holy Mysteries reside in "the hearts of the people of verification (*ahl al-taḥqīq*) and no-one is fit for them [these knowledges] except the people in [God's] special care and graced by [His] help (*ahl al-ʿināya wa 'l-tawfīq*), the followers of the straight way."

# 4

# Correspondences in Contemplation 3

The Arabic word for each of the seventy veils enumerated in the third contemplation has been transliterated below. The possible correspondences between the veils and the detailed explanation provided later in the text, in the [Letter] from the First Existence to the Second Existence, have been indicated by placing the respective number in parentheses whenever the relationship is evident. The correspondences may be suggested by the use of the same lexical root, or by semantic affinity or by symbolic analogy. Sometimes the correspondence is not clear – for example, the allusion to more than one veil may be implied in a single reference – which explains the omission of some numbers.[1]

| The Veils | [Letter] from the First Existence to the Second Existence |
|---|---|
| 1 non-existence (*ʿadam*) | Non-existence (1) preceded you, |
| 2 existence (*wujūd*) | you being (2) |
| 3 the existent (*mawjūd*) | already existent (3). |
| 4 the [primordial] covenants (*ʿuhūd*) | Then I made a covenant with you (4) |

1. See Hakim and Beneito, *Contemplaciones*, p. 31, n. 21. In the Spanish translation, the correspondences are indicated in the text. See on this theme the article by J. W. Morris, "The spiritual ascension: Ibn ʿArabi and the *miʿrāj*, Part II", *Journal of the American Oriental Society*, no. 108 (1988), pp. 73–4. He notes that there are sixty-nine different kinds of knowledge associated with the spiritual *miʿrāj*.

| | |
|---|---|
| 5 the return (*rujūʿ*) | in the Presence of Oneness, with your affirmation that "I am God and there is no divinity but Me" and you gave Me testimony of that. Then I made you return (5). |
| 6 the seas (*buḥūr*) | After that I brought you out and I cast you into the sea (6). |
| 7 the darknesses (*ẓulumāt*) | Next I flung your parts into the darknesses (7), |
| 8 yielding (*khuḍūʿ*)<br>9 instruction (*taʿlīm*) | then I sent you to them [as a messenger] (9) and they accepted you with obedience and they yielded (8). |
| 10 derivation (*ishtiqāq*) | I gave you the company and solace of a part of yourself (10), |
| 11 permission (*ibāḥa*) | whose company is licit for you (11). |
| 12 prohibition (*manʿ*) | Then I forbade you My Presence (12), |
| 13 transgression (*taʿaddī*) | but I allowed you to enter it [against My wishes] (13). |
| 14 anger (*ghaḍab*), | I became angry with you (14) |
| 15 imprisonment (*sajn*), | and I imprisoned you (15), even though you are blessed. |
| 16 letters (*ḥurūf*) | After this, I formed the letters (16) |
| 17 generation (*tawallud*) | and I preserved them for you (17).[2] |
| 18 partial death (*al-mawt al-juzʾī*) | I gave you the Pen and I sat you on your throne and you wrote on the Guarded Tablet what I wanted of you. I vivified part of you (18), |
| 19 total death (*al-mawt al-kullī*) | giving you then the plenitude of life (19). |

2. See Contemplation 3, n. 46.

| | |
|---|---|
| 20 direction (*tawjīh*) | Next I took out some parts of you, I dispersed them in the corners of the prison [of the world] (20), |
| 21 transmission (*tablīgh*) | speaking in different kinds of languages (21), |
| 22 holding fast (*i'tiṣām*)[3] | I fortified them with [the gift of] impeccability (22) |
| 23 the two feet (*qadamān*) | and seated them on their chairs (23).[4] |
| 24 universal privilege (*ikhtiṣāṣ*) | Then I singled out one of them (24) |
| 25 wrapping (*tazmīl*)[5] | for whose cause I have singled you out [too] and I strengthened him with the Words (25). |
| 26 splitting open (*shaqq*)[6]<br>27 purification (*taṭhīr*)<br>28 recomposition (*talfīq*) | I purified him from all blemish (26, 27, 28). |
| 29 interdiction (*taḥrīm*) | I forbade him to turn to the created things (29), |
| 30 sanctification (*taqdīs*) | I sanctified his place (30) |

3. This has the meaning of clinging to God, taking refuge in Him and therefore being safeguarded by Him. According to Lane, the *Tāj al-'Arūs* states: "*'iṣma al-anbiyā'* (the impeccability of the prophets) signifies God's preservation of the prophets; first, by the peculiar endowment of them with essential purity of constitution; then, by the conferring of large and highly esteemed excellences; then, by aid against opponents, and rendering their feet firm; then, by sending down upon them tranquillity (*al-sakīna*) and the preservation of their hearts, *or* minds, and adaptation to that which is right".

4. The word "chairs" comes from the same root as the *kursī*, the Footstool or Pedestal of the Throne, upon which God's two feet rest – the foot of mercy and the foot of mercy mixed with wrath. See Chittick, *Self-Disclosure*, p. xxx.

5. This refers to the beginning of the revelation of the Quran to Muhammad. He asked his wife, Khadīja, to wrap him up until the feeling of great awe left him.

6. This refers to the opening of Muhammad's chest and the purification of his heart prior to the Night Journey.

| | |
|---|---|
| 31 intercession (*shaf'*)[7] | and I granted him the right of intercession in favour of all (31). |
| 32 mounting (*imtiṭā'*) | Then I plunged him into the sea and he mounted one of his mounts (32). |
| 33 travelling (sulūk) | He journeyed by night in the instant (33) |
| 34 milk (*laban*)[8]<br>35 knocking (*qar'*)<br>36 mixing (*imtizāj*) | and I brought it down upon the Dome of Arīn (34, 35, 36). |
| 37 spirits (*arwāḥ*)<br>38 beauty (*jamāl*)<br>39 elevation (*'ulan*)<br>40 authority (*siyāda*) | Then I gave him total life (37)<br>and protected him from his partial nature (38, 39, 40) |
| 41 intimate conversation (*munājāh*) | and I addressed him (41) |
| 42 dissolution (*taḥlīl*) | from his centre (42),[9] |
| 43 reaching the end (*intihā'*)<br>44 letting go (*tark*) | saying, "On leaving (44) limitedness (43), |
| 45 love (*maḥabba*) | I will love you (45) |
| 46 removal of the intermediaries (*raf' al-wasā'iṭ*) | and on the departing of the spirits (46), |
| 47 the secret [centre] (*sirr*) | I will gladden you (47).[10] |
| 48 the chests (*ṣudūr*) | Bring out (48)[11] |

7. This word can also mean "being one of a pair".

8. According to tradition Muhammad said: "I was given a vessel full of wine, a vessel full of milk and a vessel full of honey, and I took the milk" (*Ṣaḥīḥ*, al-Bukhārī).

9. See Contemplation 3, n. 60: the "centre" is the "place of equilibrium" (*maḥall al-i'tidāl*). The word *maḥall* is derived from the same root as *taḥlīl*.

10. "The secret [centre]" (*sirr*) comes from the same root as the verb "to gladden" (*sarra*).

11. The root of the word *ṣudūr*, chests, also means to bring out.

| | |
|---|---|
| 49 veracity (*ṣiddīqiyya*), | and make manifest the heart of the veracious (49), |
| 50 irresistible power (*qahr*) | and conquer (50). |
| 51 sense of shame (*ḥayā'*) | Take the secret of life (51)[12] and entrust it to whomsoever you wish. |
| 52 boldness (*shahāma*) | Draw the sword of vengeance, with it raise your sign and with it defeat whoever opposes you (52). |
| 53 leave-taking (*inṣirām*) | Then come to Me; let your son go (53), |
| 54 inheritance (*mīrāth*) | that he may take your place (54) |
| 55 uprooting (*iṣṭilām*)[13] | and tell him to be consumed (55) |
| 56 annihilation (*fanā'*) | in annihilation (56) |
| 57 subsistence (*baqā'*) | by his subsistence (57), |
| 58 jealousy (*ghayra*) | not to be jealous (58) |
| 59 spiritual will (*himma*)<br>60 unveiling (*kashf*) | of [communicating] his revelation (60) |
| 61 contemplation (*mushāhada*) | and to contemplate Me (61) |
| 62 majesty (*jalāl*)<br>63 beauty (*jamāl*) | in the attributes (62, 63), |
| 64 disappearance of the individual essence (*dhahāb al-ʿayn*) | but not in the essences, because I am not contained by them (64). |

12. "Life" (*ḥayā*) has the same root as the "sense of shame" (*ḥayā'*).

13. Ibn ʿArabī defines *iṣṭilām* in the *Futūḥāt* (II.131) as: "the quality of distracted and rapturous love that arrives in the heart, which then rests under its power".

| | |
|---|---|
| 65 the imperceptible (*mā lā yudrak*)<br>66 the inaudible (*mā lā yusmaʿ*)<br>67 the incomprehensible (*mā lā yufham*)<br>68 the incommunicable (*mā lā yunqal*)<br>69 symbolic allusion (*ishāra*)<br>70 the whole (*kull*) | Although he may listen (66), understand (67), know, allude (69), communicate (68), particularize or summarize (70), he will not comprehend Me (65). |

# Bibliography


*The Holy Qur'ān*. Text, translation and commentary by A. Yusuf Ali. London, 1975.

Sarrāj, Abū Naṣr al-. *Luma'*. Cairo, 1960.

Addas, Claude. *Quest for the Red Sulphur*. Cambridge, 1993.

—— "Abu Madyan and Ibn 'Arabi", in *Muhyiddin Ibn 'Arabi: A Commemorative Volume*, edited by S. Hirtenstein and M. Tiernan, pp. 163–80. Shaftesbury, Dorset, 1993.

Austin, R.W.J. *Sufis of Andalusia*. Sherborne, Glos., 1988.

Benaïssa, Omar. "The Diffusion of Akbarian Teaching in Iran during the 13th and 14th Centuries", *JMIAS*, XXVI, 1999, pp. 89–109.

Beneito, Pablo. *El Secreto de los Nombres de Dios*. Murcia, 1996.

Burckhardt, Titus. *Mystical Astrology According to Ibn 'Arabī*. Aldsworth, Glos., 1977.

Chittick, William C. *The Sufi Path of Knowledge: Ibn al-'Arabī's Metaphysics of Imagination*. Albany, New York, 1989.

—— *The Self-Disclosure of God: Principles of Ibn al-'Arabī's Cosmology*. Albany, New York, 1998.

Chodkiewicz, Michel. *Les Illuminations de La Mecque / The Meccan Illuminations*. See under *Al-Futūḥāt al-Makkiyya*.

—— *An Ocean Without Shore: Ibn Arabi, The Book, and the Law*. Albany, New York, 1993.

—— *Seal of the Saints: Prophethood and Sainthood in the Doctrine of Ibn 'Arabī*. Cambridge, 1993.

Corbin, Henry. *Creative Imagination in the Sufism of Ibn 'Arabī*. Princeton, 1969.

—— *Spiritual Body and Celestial Earth*. Princeton, 1977.

Elmore, G. "The *Uwaysī* Spirit of Autodidactic Sainthood as the 'Breath of the Merciful'", *JMIAS*, XXVIII, 2000, pp. 35–56.

Hakim, Souad. *Al-Mu'jam al-ṣūfī*. Beirut, 1981.

—— and Beneito, Pablo. *Las Contemplaciones de los Misterios*. See under Ibn 'Arabī.

Hirtenstein, Stephen. *The Unlimited Mercifier: The Spiritual Life and Thought of Ibn 'Arabī*. Oxford, 1999.

Ibn al-'Arīf. *Maḥāsin al-majālis*. Edited by M. Asín Palacios. Paris, 1933.

Ibn 'Arabī, Muḥyīddīn, *Kitāb Ayyām al-sha'n*. In *Rasā'il Ibn 'Arabi*. Hyderabad, 1948.

—— *Las Contemplaciones de los Misterios*. Introduction, edition, translation and notes by S. Hakim and P. Beneito. Murcia, reprinted 1996.

—— *Al-Futūḥāt al-Makkiyya*. Edited by O. Yahia. Cairo, 1990. Selected passages translated and commented on in *Les Illuminations de La Mecque/Meccan*

*Illuminations* by M. Chodkiewicz (ed.), with W. C. Chittick, C. Chodkiewicz, D. Gril and J. W. Morris. Paris, 1988. Now translated into English as *Meccan Revelations*. Volume I, 2002, Volume II, 2004. [French to English translation by David Streight.] New York.
—— *Al-Futūḥāt al-Makkiyya*. Beirut, n.d.
—— *Ihtiṣār sīrat rasūl Allāh*. Edited by M. Kamāl al-Dīn ʿIzz al-Dīn, Beirut, 1987.
—— *Ismail Hakki Bursevi's Translation of and Commentary on Fusus al-Hikam by Muhyiddin Ibn ʿArabi*. Rendered into English by B. Rauf. 4 vols. Oxford, 1986–91.
—— *The Wisdom of the Prophets*. (Extracts from the *Fuṣūṣ al-ḥikam*.) Translated by T. Burckhardt / A. Culme-Seymour. Aldsworth, Glos., 1975.
—— *Kitāb al-Isfār ʿan natāʾij al-asfār*. Edited and translated by D. Gril under the title *Le Dévoilement des Effets du Voyage*. Combas, 1994.
—— *Kitāb al-Isrāʾ ilā l-maqām al-asrā*. Critical edition and notes by S. Hakim. Beirut, 1988.
—— *Kitāb mashāhid l-asrār al-qudsiyya*. Edited, translated into French and presented by S. Ruspoli under the title *Le Livre des Contemplations divines*. Arles, 1999.
—— *Kitāb al-Mīm wa 'l-wāw wa 'l-nūn*. In *Rasāʾil Ibn ʿArabi*. Hyderabad, 1948.
—— *The Seven Days of the Heart*. (The *Awrād al-usbuʿ* or *Wird*.) Translated and presented by P. Beneito and S. Hirtenstein. Oxford, 2000.
—— *Tanazzulāt al-Mawṣiliyya*. Cairo, 1961.
—— *Tarjumān al-ashwāq*. Translated by R.A. Nicholson. London, reprinted 1978.
—— *Wird*. Oxford, 1979.
Lane, E. W. *An Arabic–English Lexicon*. Cambridge, reprinted 1984.
Lory, Pierre. "The Symbolism of Letters and Language in the Work of Ibn ʿArabī", *JMIAS*, XXIII, 1998, pp. 32–42.
Morris, James, W. "The Spiritual Ascension: Ibn ʿArabi and the *Miʿrāj*, Part II", *Journal of the American Oriental Society*, 108, 1988.
—— "Ibn ʿArabī's Spiritual Ascension". In *Les Illuminations de La Mecque/The Meccan Illuminations*, edited by M. Chodkiewicz. Paris, 1988, pp. 351–438.
Niffarī, Muḥammad Ibn ʿAbdi 'l-Jabbār, al-. *The Mawāqif and Mukhāṭabāt*. Translated by A.J. Arberry. London, reprinted 1978.
Safi, Omid, "Did the Two Oceans Meet?", *JMIAS*, XXVI, 1999, pp. 55–88.
Sitt al-ʿAjam (Sitt ʿAǧam) bint al-Nafis al-Baghdādiyya, *Sharḥ al-mashāhid al-qudsiyya*. Edited by Bakri Aladdin and Souad Hakim, IFPO, Damascus, 2004.
Taher, Hamed. "Sainthood and Prophecy", *Alif*, 5, Cairo, 1985, pp. 7–38.
Twinch, Cecilia, "Muḥyiddīn Ibn ʿArabī and the Interior Wisdom", in *Los dos Horizontes* (*Textos sobre Ibn Al ʿArabī*). Edited by Alfonso Carmona Gonzalez, Editora Regional de Murcia, 1992.
—— "Penetrating Meaning", *JMIAS*, XX, 1996, pp. 67–79.
Wensinck, A.J., Mensing, J.P. and Brugman, J. *Concordance et indices de la tradition musulmane*. Leiden, 1936–69.
Yahia, Osman, *Histoire et classification de l'oeuvre d'Ibn ʿArabī*, including the Répertoire Général (R.G.) of his works. Damascus, 1964.